DECORATIVE PAINTING
with GRETCHEN CAGLE

GRETCHEN CAGLE, CDA

NORTH LIGHT BOOKS
CINCINNATI, OHIO

Biography

Gretchen Cagle, after twenty-three years of tole and decorative painting, continues to be one of the industry's leading designers, as well as a teacher, publisher and author. The thirteen books and six videos in her highly acclaimed *Heart to Heart* series and her flair and approach to color and design have inspired thousands of decorative artists to paint. Countless others have admired and painted Gretchen's designs, which have appeared in *Good Housekeeping, The Decorative Artist's Workbook, The Decorative Painter, Craftworks for the Home, Family Circle/Great Ideas Christmas Helps* and *Redbook*.

Gretchen has received recognition as a Certified Decorative Artist through the National Society of Tole and Decorative Painters, an organization of thirty thousand members. She was the 1985-1986 president and received the coveted Distinguished Service Award in 1994.

Gretchen maintains an active seminar schedule. In addition to teaching nationally and internationally, she teaches weekly classes in Tulsa, Oklahoma.

Gretchen is actively involved in her publishing company, a leading producer of instructional material within the decorative painting industry. Over twenty-five of the most recognized decorative artists in the United States have chosen her to publish and distribute their books.

Decorative Painting With Gretchen Cagle. Copyright © 1996 by Gretchen Cagle. Printed and bound in Hong Kong. All rights reserved. No part of this book may be reproduced in any form or by any electronic or mechanical means including information storage and retrieval systems without permission in writing from the publisher, except by a reviewer, who may quote brief passages in a review. Published by North Light Books, an imprint of F&W Publications, Inc., 1507 Dana Avenue, Cincinnati, Ohio 45207. (800) 289-0963. First edition.

00 99 98 97 96   5 4 3 2 1

Library of Congress Cataloging-in-Publication Data

Cagle, Gretchen
    Decorative painting with Gretchen Cagle / by Gretchen Cagle.
      p. cm.
    Includes index.
    ISBN 0-89134-733-X (alk. paper)
    1. Painting. 2. Tole Painting. 3. Decoration and ornament—Plant forms. 4. Decoration and ornament, Rustic. I. Title.
TT385.C34 1996
745.7'23 dc20

95-26069
CIP

Edited by Pam Seyring
Cover designed by Sandy Conopeotis Kent
Interior designed by Angela Lennert Wilcox

The materials in this compilation appeared in the following pamphlets previously published by Gretchen Cagle Publications, Inc. *Heart to Heart . . . & All Things Country; Heart to Heart . . . Country Collection; Heart to Heart . . . Decorated With Elegance; Heart to Heart . . . Essence of Summer; Heart to Heart . . . Floral Accents; Heart to Heart . . . Lavished With Love; Heart to Heart . . . Painted Treasures; Heart to Heart . . . Rose Petals, Heart Strings and Other Things; Heart to Heart . . . With Simple Pleasures; Simply Toled*.

Contents

CHAPTER I

Daisies, Geraniums, Pansies and Tulips

CHAPTER II

A Bounty of Blooms

Before You Begin

Brushes

Winsor & Newton Series 710—Use these red sable, short-bristled flats (sometimes called "brights") in sizes 2 through 12 for color application and blending. All brushes should have sharp, clean chisel edges that hold together even after applying and blending paint. Poor edges will yield fuzzy edges on design elements and will be difficult to blend with.

Winsor & Newton Series 3A—Use these small red sable rounds in sizes 0 to 1 to create all line work, pollen dots and for small, detailed areas.

You can substitute any excellent quality red sable flats, liners or round brushes for the brushes mentioned above. Synthetics may also be used, however, they quickly become saturated with paint and painting mediums due to their lack of resiliency. Have several of each size available if you decide to use synthetic brushes. When a brush no longer snaps back to its original flat, chisel-edged shape, clean it in odorless brush cleaner and lay it aside for several days before using it again.

Paints

Most of the designs in this book are painted with Winsor & Newton Alkyd or Oil Colours. Oils and alkyds are totally compatible; therefore, the same mediums and varnishes may be used with both, and they may be used together on the same palette and inter-mixed with each other. Since alkyd colors dry quicker than oil colors, the higher the proportion of alkyd color in a mixture, the quicker the colors will dry. If you're using an all-alkyd palette, the colors will be workable for approximately

Paint Palettes

Use the following key for abbreviations:

	Winsor & Newton Alkyd or Oils	Liquitex Oils
AC	Alizarin Crimson	Same
BLK	Ivory Black	Same
BR		Barn Red
BS	Burnt Sienna	Same
BU	Burnt Umber	Same
CBH	Cerulean Blue Hue	
CL	Cadmium Lemon	Cadmium Yellow Light
CO	Cadmium Orange	Same
CoB	Cobalt Blue	
CoBH	Cobalt Blue Hue	
COG		Chromium Oxide Green
CoVH	Cobalt Violet Hue	
CRD	Cadmium Red Deep	
CRL	Cadmium Red Light	Same
CRM	Cadmium Red Medium	
CYD	Cadmium Yellow Deep	
CYL	Cadmium Lemon	Cadmium Yellow Light
CYM	Cadmium Yellow Medium	Same or Cadmium Yellow Deep
DP	Dioxazine Purple	Same
FT	Flesh Tint	
FU	French Ultramarine	Ultramarine Blue
IR	Indian Red	Same
LRO	Light Red Oxide or Light Red	
Mauve		Mauve
NY		Naples Yellow Hue
NYH	Naples Yellow Hue	Same

PB	Prussian Blue	Same
PG	Paynes Grey	
RM	Rose Madder	
RS	Raw Sienna	Same
RU	Raw Umber	Same
SG	Sap Green	Sap Green Permanent
TW	Titanium White	Same
UB		Ultramarine Blue
VR	Venetian Red	
YO	Yellow Ochre	Same

Rembrandt Oils

BMA	Brownish Madder
NYD	Naples Yellow Deep Extra
NYL	Naples Yellow Light Extra

Grumbacher Oils

GL	Geranium Lake
MAUVE	Mauve
TYG	Thalo Yellow Green

Winsor & Newton Acrylics

AC	Alizarin Crimson
OG	Olive Green
TW	Titanium White
UB	Ultramarine Blue
YO	Yellow Ochre

CeramCoat Acrylic Colors

ACF	AC Flesh
FB	Fjord Blue
C	Cayenne
BY	Butter Yellow

forty-five minutes, at which point they may become too tacky for you to do any additional blending. If you use an all-alkyd palette, work and complete small areas of the design at a time. Alkyd colors will be completely dry in eighteen hours and will often be dry in ten to twelve hours, depending on climactic conditions and air movement over the painting surface. Slightly more transparent than oils, alkyds are wonderful for glazing and staining.

Miscellaneous Supplies

Winsor & Newton Blending & Glazing Medium
Odorless brush cleaner
Disposable palette paper
Tracing paper
Felt tip marker
Woven paper towels
Gray graphite paper
White graphite paper
Stylus
Masking tape
Facial tissue

Background Preparation

1. Seal all wood surfaces with Designs From the Heart Wood Sealer or any other quality brush-on wood sealer.
2. Sand wood surfaces when the sealer is dry.
3. Paint the item with acrylic or stain it using the background color of your choice.
4. Spray with Krylon Matte Finish before applying your pattern.

Transferring the Pattern

1. Precisely trace the main design elements with a felt tip pen. Do not trace shading and tendrils or vein lines and stems on leaves.
2. Correctly position the tracing on your painting surface.
3. Secure tracing with masking tape.
4. Slide a graphite sheet under the tracing.
5. Using a stylus, trace the pattern onto the surface with light pressure.

Terminology

Accent—Usually a mid value color used to add interest and help harmonize the overall composition.

Base—Fill in the entire area with a solid color.

Blocking in—Laying in the initial statement by a broad indication of tone, color and line.

Buff—Colors that build good variations among design items and are applied with short, choppy strokes. Blend with the brush, pulling one color into another.

Dark Area—Usually refers to color applied in shadows. With flowers, it is generally positioned beneath the petals. With fruit or other round objects, it normally takes the shape of a crescent and is positioned opposite the light source.

Double Load Your Brush—Same as side load except that one color is loaded onto one side of the brush and another color is loaded onto the other side of the brush.

Glazing—Oil-based medium applied over a dry area to facilitate application of additional color.

Highlight—An area of brightest or most intense value on a design element. Color is built in layers, with the area covered by each application becoming smaller and lighter:
1. Load your brush with the desired color.
2. Release paint in the highlight area.
3. Softly blend only the outside edges between each color application.
4. Repeat using the next lightest value.
5. Soften over the entire highlight area to complete.

Light Area—The lightest color used to complete the block-in of an object. It is not as light, bright nor as intense as the highlight that is normally positioned over the light area.

Marbling—In painting, a mingling of colors to form an irregular pattern, such as that found in marble.

Mid Value—Color between the dark and light areas of a design element. If several mid values are listed, apply the darkest color next to the dark area, blend, and apply and blend each successive color next to the previously applied color.

Overcolor—Refers to the stroking of a color over an undercolor, usually to create daisy or rose petals.

Reflected Light—Where the crescent opposite the light source on a round object does not touch the outside edge, usually painted a mid value, often with a BLK + TW or FU + TW tint.

Scumbling—Refers to the application of a scant amount of color to a dry surface to which no glazing medium has been applied. Color is applied with an old, worn brush that is then dry-wiped and used to blend or soften the color into the surrounding colors.

Shade—Color used to deepen shadow within a dark area of the design element. On a round top object, it is applied diagonally opposite the light source. On overlapping objects, it is used to deepen the triangular areas that form in the overlap of the elements:
1. Side load your brush.
2. Place the shade value in dark areas.
3. "Walk" the shade value out into the body of object.
4. Wipe your brush.
5. Softly blend only the outside edge.

Side Load Your Brush—Load one corner or one side of the brush with color. Before applying it to the surface, the color should be blended on a clean area of the palette so that it is evenly distributed through the loaded side of the brush. When painting with a properly loaded brush, there should not be a hard or very well-defined edge to the color break.

Tint—Sometimes a pure color mixed with white, such as TW + FU, is used in the reflected light area of a round object. When a tint is not mixed with white, it means the same as "accent."

Undercolor—The first application of a color or a combination of colors applied to an object. It normally forms soft, shadowing areas of color on the object. For instance, undercolor may be applied under daisy or rose petals before you actually stroke on the petals. When petals are stroked over it, the undercolor bleeds through slightly.

"Walk" Color Out—Gradually soften and blend color so that it flows without a color break from one area of the design into another area.

Wipe Your Brush—Fold a very soft paper towel into several layers. Position the brush between the layers and gently press and then pull the bristles through the towel to remove any excess paint. Normally done after applying color but before blending or when changing colors.

Color Notes

Plus (+) indicates that colors should be brush-mixed together on the palette:

1. From the puddle of colors, pull out a small amount of the first color listed.
2. Work it into the brush.
3. With the now loaded brush, pull out from the puddle the second color listed.
4. Work it into the brush, blending the colors together on the palette.

Repeat these steps until the desired color is achieved. Do not overload the brush. It is not necessary to mix all the color for one area. Variation will add interest.

Dash (-) indicates a dry wipe technique:

1. Apply the first color or combination listed.
2. Dry wipe the brush. (Never clean your brush with turpentine when changing colors.)
3. If you're making a dramatic change in value, neutralize the dry-wiped brush with YO or TW.
4. Dry wipe your brush several more times.
5. Apply the next color or combination listed on top of the first. Each application of color laid on another should be smaller in size than the area of previously applied color.
6. Blend before applying the next color.

When a dash is used with tints in mid value areas, apply colors adjacent to each other rather than on top of one another.

Parenthesis ( ) indicate the color is optional. Use sparingly on some objects for variation.

Painting Techniques

When using alkyd colors, it is important to use an ample amount of paint because of their faster drying time. Load the brush fully with color so that the inner and outer bristles of the brush are evenly saturated. Apply color so that the background of the surface is evenly coated and not visible through the paint; however, do not use so much paint that it forms ridges. Apply the color with short, choppy, overlapping strokes, moving the brush in all directions. Apply each color as listed, and then blend with soft pressure strokes before applying another color. When blending colors, allow the brush to straddle over the color break and, with the same brush-stroking technique, soften the color only where it touches its neighboring color. Blend only enough to merge the colors, alleviating any defined break between them. It is not necessary to blend clear across a previously applied color. Allowing a color to blend with a color that is not adjacent to it will result in over blending and loss of value.

When the paint begins to tack up or lifts as a color is applied on top of it, it will be necessary to apply and blend new applications of paint with heavier pressure. The pressure will push fresh paint under the drier layer of paint on top and allow it to blend with the wetter colors underneath. If the color becomes too dry before completing work in a specific area, allow the color to dry to the touch and then apply any additional color using a glazing technique.

Oil colors should be applied to the surface in the same manner as alkyds, but because of their extended drying time, use less paint. Apply small amounts of color to the surface and stretch it to cover the design element.

Regardless of the paint of choice, always apply the highlight or lighter values to a darker value firmly and with pressure, thus assuring maximum value change within that area.

Glazing Techniques

Through the use of glazing techniques, you can continue to work easily over a surface that dried before you completed the work. You can also enhance or change any previously painted area that could benefit from additional work. Glazing techniques are especially well suited for strengthening the dark shadow area, building stronger highlights and glints, as well as adding tints to the reflected light areas of a design element.

Glazing must be done on a surface that is completely dry to the touch. Remember that even though the surface feels dry, the underneath layers of paint may still be fragile. Glazing techniques are done with oil-based painting mediums, which may act as a solvent to any paint that is not completely cured and bonded to the surface. If paint lifts from the surface, allow additional drying time before continuing to work.

To glaze, wet the surface with a thin coat of Winsor & Newton Blending and Glazing Medium or any other oil-based painting medium. If the medium puddles, position a single layer of facial tissue on the surface and tap it with your fingertip. Load a small amount of the desired color into the brush and apply it to the glazed surface. Dry-wipe the brush on a paper towel, and with soft pressure strokes, blend the color into the wet medium. Remember that value changes should be gradual and without any line of demarcation between applications of colors. To build a very strong and intense highlight over a darker area, it may be necessary to glaze the area. Apply a color similar to the dried surface color, blending it into the medium. Then—while that color is still wet—apply a lighter, more intense value, blending it into the previously applied color. This technique is especially important when you're adding paint over a stronger or darker color that may appear chalky or milky after blending.

Daisies, Geraniums, Pansies and Tulips

Daisies & Geraniums

If you love summer gardens, then you must love daisies and geraniums. Daisies fill the garden with dancing, white, lacy blossoms that cheer the soul, while geraniums add brightness and color. This summer duo is sure to please the eye!

Background

Seal the surfaces with Designs from the Heart Wood Sealer and sand when dry. Paint the entire surface, including the frame, with any black acrylic paint. Paint the insets for the lettering and the inner edge of the frame with DecoArt Hauser Medium Green and then spray with Krylon Matte Finish. Antique the green areas with black alkyd color. For extra interest, gold leaf the frames with variegated green leafing that has been antiqued with black alkyd color.

Palette

Winsor & Newton Alkyd Colours: Alizarin Crimson, Cadmium Red Medium, Cadmium Red Light, Yellow Ochre, Cadmium Orange, Titanium White, Ivory Black, Naples Yellow Hue, Dioxazine Purple, Prussian Blue, Cadmium Lemon, Cadmium Yellow Medium and Light Red Oxide.

Refer to page 16 for geranium notes.

Daisies

Undercoat . . . . .BLK
Overcoat . . . . . .TW + NYH
Shade . . . . .BLK
Highlight. . . . . .TW
Tint . . . . .LRO + NYH
. . . . .LRO + AC

Daisy Centers

Base. . . . . .YO + CYM
Shade . . . . .AC + small amt.
BLK
Highlight. . . . . .CYM
. . . . .CL + TW
Tint . . . . .TW + AC
Pollen . . . . .BLK
. . . . .CYM

Daisy Leaves

Base. . . . . .CL + BLK +
TW + PB
Shade . . . . .Base mix +
BLK + PB
Highlight. . . . . .TW + CL
. . . . .TW + PB
. . . . .TW
Tint . . . . .LRO + CYM

Lettering

Base. . . . . .CRM
Shade . . . . .AC + BLK
Highlight. . . . . .CRL
. . . . .CRL + NYH
Shadow . . . . . .BLK + AC

Daisies & Geraniums

Refer to page 14 for background preparation.

Lettering

Base . . . . .CRM
Shade . . . . . . .AC + BLK
Highlight . . . . .CRL
. . . . .CRL + NYH
Shadow . . . . . .BLK + AC

Light Geranium (Top)

Dark Area . . . . .CRM + AC
Light Area . . . . .CRL
Highlight . . . . . .CO + TW
Shade . . . . . . .AC + CRM
Tint . . . . .TW + BLK + AC
Pollen Dots . . . .BLK
. . . . .Green leaf
mixtures

Mid Value Geranium (Middle)

Dark Area . . . . .AC
Mid Value . . . . .CRM
Light Area . . . . .CRM + YO
Highlight . . . . . .NYH + CRL
. . . . .NYH + CRM
Shade . . . . . . .AC + BLK
Tint . . . . .AC + DP + TW
. . . . .CO

Pollen Dots . . . . .BLK

. . . . .Green leaf
mixtures

Dark Geranium (Bottom)

Dark Area . . . . . .AC + PB
Light Area . . . . . .AC + CRM
Highlight. . . . . . .CRM + CRL
Shade . . . . .AC + PB
Tint . . . . .AC + PB + TW
Pollen Dots . . . .BLK-Green leaf
mixtures

Geranium Leaves

Base. . . . . .CL + TW + BLK
Shade . . . . .Base mix +
BLK + PB
Highlight. . . . . . .Base mix +
CL + TW
. . . . .TW
Tint . . . . .PB + TW
. . . . .CRL + YO
. . . . .Green mixes
+ AC

Daisies & Geraniums

Base the leaves keeping the upper leaf lighter in value.

Begin by placing in a collar of BLK outside the flower center so that it extends ⅔'s the distance to the petal edge. Overstroke the petals with one or two strokes per petal. Be sure to let up on the pressure as you pull toward the flower center.

Barely blend those petals with double strokes to eliminate any gaps. Tuck shading into the overlaps and softly blend.

Shade at the stem end of the leaf and in any overlaps. Create a strong shadow above the center vein line.

Apply the first application of highlight and blend towards outer edge to create the growth pattern.

Highlight along the exposed edge of the top petals and strengthen the shading if necessary.

Tint the outer edges of the petals. Build a very strong highlight in the center area of each petal. The combination of tints on the tips, strong highlight in the center and shading bleeding from the center gives the feeling that the petal arches forward catching light.

Apply final highlight, tints, and the vein. Use the base mix to paint the vein within the shaded center area.

Position the dark area on the right side in the form of a crescent and then apply the mid and light values working toward the left side of the flower. Barely blend the colors together. Using a stylus, scratch out the petal shapes that form each flowerlet within the blossom. With the highlight color, outline the petals and blend leaving the base color showing at the center of each petal. Use the lightest highlight color in the lighter areas and the darker highlight color within the darker area of the blossom. If necessary, add shading to develop stronger darks at each flower center and in the overlaps. Many of the petals have tints placed on them. Tint the petals closest to the light source with the warmer tints and those furthest away from the light source with the cool tints.

Base the leaves and then apply shading in an irregular circle inside the leaf. Pull out streaks similar to those done on pansies. Build stronger highlights along the leaf edge and form light streaks of highlight over the darker streaks. Tint along the leaf edge and in overlaps.

Spring Beauties

Undercolor

Light Area

Dark Area

Overcolor

Highlight

Shade

Tint

Highlight

Tint

Dark Streak

Light Streaks

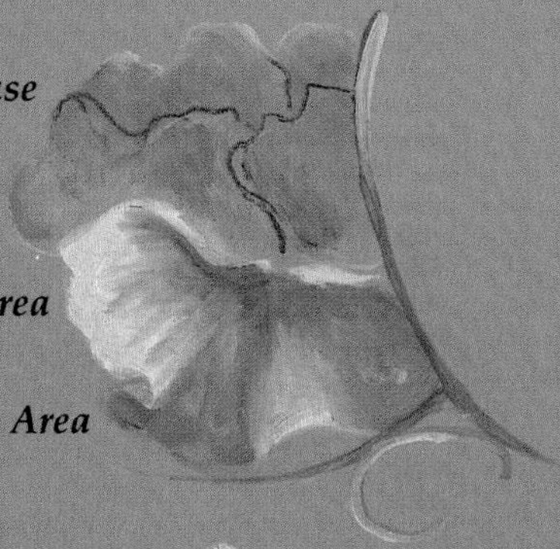

Base

Light Area

Dark Area

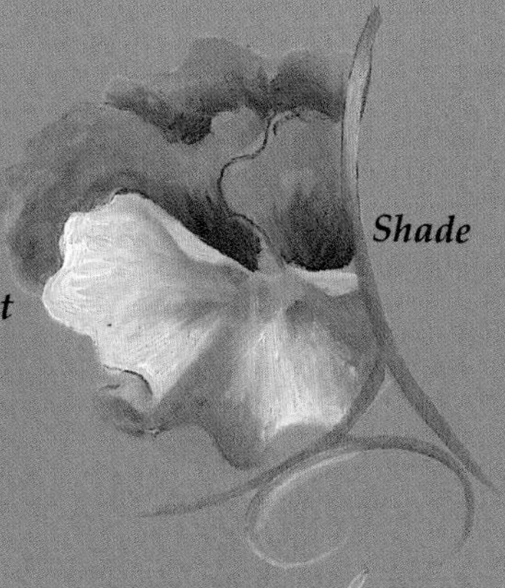

Highlight

Shade

Highlight

Tint

Tint

Dark Streaks

Light Streaks

Surface available from
Wood You Imagine, P.O. Box 691632,
Tulsa, OK 74169-1632.

Spring Beauties

Prepare the background for this un-usual swing-arm jewelry box with Folk Art Porcelain Blue. The outer edge of the swing-arm is gold leafed.

Daisies

Undercolor . . . .PG + CoBH
Overcolor . . . . .TW + small amt. NYH
Shade . . . . .PG + CoBH
Highlight. . . . . .TW
Tint . . . . .CL + NYH

Daisy Centers

Base. . . . . .YO
Shade . . . . . . .AC + DP
Highlight. . . . . .CL + TW
. . . . .TW
Tint . . . . .CoBH + TW
Pollen . . . . . . .PG
. . . . .CoBH + TW

Left Pansy

Front Petal

Light Area . . . .TW + NYH + small amt. CL
Dark Area . . . . .CoBH + TW + PG
. . . . .small amt. CoBH
Highlight. . . . . .TW + CL
Tint . . . . .CO
Dark Streaks . . .AC + DP
Light Streaks . . .CO

Back Petals

Base. . . . . .TW + CoBH + PG + DP
Shade . . . . . . .PG + DP + CoBH
Highlight. . . . . .TW
Tint . . . . .TW + CL
(applied over highlights)

Right Pansy

Light Area . . . .TW + CL + NYH
Dark Area . . . . .TW + PG + CoBH + DP

Shade . . . . . . .Dark mix + CoBH + PG
Highlight. . . . . .TW + small amt. CL
Tint . . . . .AC-CO
Dark Streaks . . .AC + DP + PG
Light Streaks . . .CO

Leaves

Base. . . . . .CL + CoBH + PG + TW
Shade . . . . . . .Base mix + PG + CoBH

Highlight. . . . . .CL + TW
. . . . .TW
Tint . . . . .Flower Colors

Butterflies

Base. . . . . .TW + NYH
Shade . . . . . . .CL + NYH
Tint . . . . .CoBH + PG + TW

Strokework

Base. . . . . .YO
Highlight. . . . . .CL + TW

©1991
Hutchins

For my Valentine

For my Valentine

© 1987

For my Valentine

Say "I care" with this special valentine painting to give at any time. Who can resist the old fashioned sentiment conveyed by a lacy nosegay filled with spring's glory and then wrapped with a ribbon and tied with a heart?

The background is painted with Delta Old Parchment and then antiqued with the coral colors from the palette. When painting, start with the nosegay and then move to the tulips, leaves, heart, ribbon and filler flowers.

Nosegay and Ruffle on Heart
    Base..........TW + YO
    Shade ....TW + FU + BLK
    Highlight......TW
    Tint ....Flower Colors
    Detail.........BLK + FU + TW
    Keep the base soft and transparent, allowing some background to be visible through the nosegay.

Upper Right and Extreme Left Tulip
    Base..........YO + CYM
    Shade ....CRL + AC-
                AC + IR
    Highlight......TW + CL + CRL
                (soft shell pink)
    ....TW + CL
    Tint ....TW + BLK + FU

Lower Right Tulip
    Base..........TW + CYM +
                CRL (pale warm
                pink)
    Shade ....CRL-IR
    Highlight......TW + CL-TW
    Tint ....CYM + TW-
                TW + BLK + FU

Lower Left Tulip and Ribbon
    Base..........CRM + TW +
                small amt.
                YO + small amt.
                CL
    Shade ....IR + AC
    Highlight......TW + CL
    Tint ....TW + FU + BLK

Upper Left Tulip
    Base..........TW + CRL + YO
                (soft shell pink)
    Shade ....CRM + AC-
                AC + IR
    Highlight......TW
    Tint ....CYM-BLK +
                TW + FU

Heart
    Base..........TW + YO
    Shade ....TW + YO + CRL
    Highlight......TW
    Tint ....Base mix + IR

Resting Area
    ....FU + BLK + TW

Filler Flowers
    Base..........CRL + YO + TW
                (add turp)
    Highlight......CL + TW-TW
    Tint ....BLK + TW

Leaves
    Base..........BLK + CL + TW
                (pale green)
    Shade ....Base mix + BLK
    Highlight......TW
    Tint ....Flower colors

Nosegay

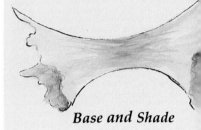

Base and Shade

Upper Right

Base

Lower Right

Base

Lower Left

Base

Upper Left

Base

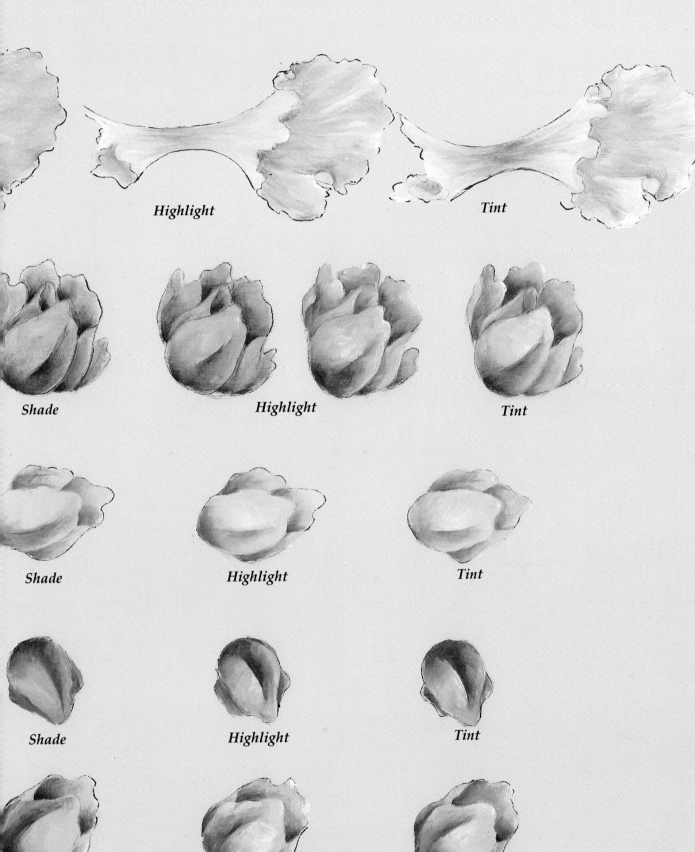

Highlight

Tint

Shade

Highlight

Tint

Shade

Highlight

Tint

Shade

Highlight

Tint

Shade

Highlight

Tint

29

Amber Beauties

Light Pansy

Light Area

Tint

Highlight

Dark Pansy

Dark Streaks

Light Streaks

Waterdrop

Base

Highlight

Shade

Light Area
"C" Stroke
TW + CYL

Blend

Shade
Dark Value
of Background

Blend

Highlight
Glint

31

Amber Beauties

The key to this beautiful painting is creating the focal point, an area the eye is drawn to and upon which it can comfortably rest. When a pattern contains many design elements, it is important to remember that the design can become very busy and lack emphasis unless you follow a few simple rules. The focal point of a design is created through the use of color, contrast and detail. Notice that the lightest pansy is nestled next to the darkest pansy, providing not only contrast of values but also the use of two different color families. Detail in this area of the design includes the flips on the front petals and the streaks of dark color within each pansy. Be sure that as you move away from this focal point the colors become duller and contrast less with the background or that they repeat the background colors.

The background is prepared with Delta Mocha. The outer band to the lid has been painted with Terra Cotta and then antiqued with Geranium Lake plus Burnt Umber.

Light Pansy

Light Area . . . . .NYD + NY
Tint . . . . .LRO + CO-CO
. . . . .YO + RS (in
            indentations)
Highlight . . . . . .NYL + CYL-TW
Dark Streaks . . .BS + GL + BU
Light Streaks . . .NY

Dark Pansy

Three Front Petals

Base . . . . .LRO
Highlight . . . . . .NY-NYD-NYL
Dark Streaks . . .GL + BU-BU
Light Streaks . . .CO

Back Petals

Base . . . . .GL + LRO
Shade . . . . .GL + BU-BU
Highlight . . . . . .CRL-NY

Dark Tulip

Base . . . . .GL + RS
Shade . . . . . . .GL + BU
Highlight . . . . .LRO + CO-YO
Tint . . . . .BLK + TW

Light Tulip

Dark Area . . . . .CO + LRO
Light Area . . . . .NYD + NY
Shade . . . . .GL + RS
. . . . .BU + CYL (over
            GL + RS at stem)
Highlight . . . . . .TW + small amt.
            CYL
Tint . . . . .CO + LRO-NY
. . . . .BLK + TW

Red-tipped Tulip

Base . . . . .NY + NYD
Shade . . . . .RS + CRL
. . . . .RS + GL + BU
Apply to overlapping areas as well as on tips.
Highlight . . . . . .NYL-CYL + TW
Tint . . . . .BLK + TW

Upper Daisy

Understroke . . .BU + CYL +
            small amt. GL
Overstroke . . . .NYD + CYL-
            CYL + TW

Upper Daisy Center

Base . . . . .YO
Shade . . . . . . .RS + GL
. . . . .GL + BU
Highlight . . . . . .CO-CYL-NYL
Dots . . . . .BU-CO

Lower Daisy

Understroke . . .BU + CYL
Overstroke . . . .NYD + CYL
Tint . . . . .CO-LRO

Lower Daisy Center

Base . . . . .RS
Shade . . . . .GL + BU
Highlight . . . . . .NYL

Leaves

Dark Area . . . . . BU + CYL

Mid Value . . . . . YO in some
leaves

Light Area . . . . . Dark mix +
CYL + TW

Highlight . . . . . . BLK + TW

. . . . CYL + TW

. . . . TW

Shade . . . . Dark mix + GL or

. . . . Dark mix + BU

© 1984

Lilac Lace

Background

Seal with Designs From the Heart Wood Sealer and then sand. Basecoat the entire surface with Americana Taupe. Wet the surface with DecoArt Control Medium and sponge lightly with any off-white acrylic. When dry, spray lightly with Krylon Matte Finish.

Palette

Winsor & Newton Alkyd Colours: Flesh Tint, Titanium White, Cadmium Red Medium, Cobalt Violet Hue, Ivory Black, Alizarin Crimson, Dioxazine Purple, French Ultramarine, Cadmium Red Deep and Cadmium Lemon.

Pink Tulip

```
Base. . . . . . . . . .FT + TW + CRM
Shade . . . . . . . .CRM + CoVH
. . . . . . . . . . . . .CoVH + small
                      amts. BLK & AC
Highlight. . . . . .TW
Tint . . . . . . . . .TW + DP +
                      FU + small amt.
                      BLK
. . . . . . . . . . . .Use various
                      mixtures.
```

Lilac Tulips

```
Dark Area . . . . .CoVH + CRD
. . . . . . . . . . . .CoVH + CRM
Mid Value . . . . .TW + CoVH +
                      Pink Tulip Base
Light Area . . . . .TW + BLK +
                      CoVH + DP
Shade . . . . . . . .CoVH + BLK
. . . . . . . . . . . .CoVH +
                      BLK + AC
Highlight. . . . . .TW
Tint . . . . . . . . .DP + FU + TW
. . . . . . . . . . . .BLK + TW
. . . . . . . . . . . .AC + CRD
```

Paint the upper lilac tulip using the same colors as for the lower but with less CRM and CRD in the mixtures. Add additional TW to the light area mixture.

Leaves

```
Base. . . . . . . . .TW + CL + BLK
Shade . . . . . . . .BLK + CoVH +
                      small amt. Base
                      mix
Highlight. . . . . .TW
Tint . . . . . . . . .Flower colors
```

Filler

```
Dark . . . . . . . . .DP + FU +
                      BLK + TW
Mid Value . . . . .TW +
                      CoVH + DP
Light . . . . . . . . .TW + BLK
Highlight. . . . . .TW
```

Pink Tulip: Apply Basecoat and first value shading
Lilac Tulip: Apply Dark, Mid Value and Light area
Filler Flowers: Apply Dark value with thinned pain

Pink Tulip: Apply second value Shading and Highlight.
Lilac Tulip: Apply Shading and Highlight.
Filler Flowers: Add Mid Value with thinned paint.

Tulips: Strengthen highlights and add tints.
Filler Flowers: Apply light value using less
thinner. Highlight using TW from the tube.

The box for Lilac Lace is available from Art Craft Wood, Box 75, Highway 69A, Crestline, KS 66728, (316) 389-2574.

Grace & Charm

Background Drape

Shade   Base

Swan

Base

Shade

Dark Area

Light Area

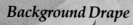

Base

Table Cloth

Base

Shade

Basket

Dark Area

Light Area

Shade

Background Drape

Tint   Highlight

Swan

Highlight

Tint

Shade

Highlight

Tint

Table Cloth

Highlight

Tint

Basket

Shade

Highlight

Highlight

Grace & Charm

Keep the mood of this painting soft and romantic by starting with a wash of water and DecoArt Jade Green acrylic over the entire box except for the heart inset, which is painted with a soft white acrylic. When the painting is completed be sure to add PG antiquing under the tablecloth, on the upper left and lower right of the lid, and around the lower edge of the bottom of the box. Add TW antiquing on the upper right of the lid. The heart is splotched with green mixtures from the leaves and accented with PG.

When you paint the drape behind the swan, be sure to keep it soft and delicate with only minimal value changes from the background. Allow it to fade away to the right behind the tulip basket.

Swan

Base	.TW + NYH
Shade	.RU + TW + PG
Highlight	.TW
Tint	.NYH + TW + small amt. AC

Eye & Beak

Base	.PG
Highlight	.TW

Basket

Dark Area	.AC + NYH
Light Area . . . , .	.FT
Shade	.AC + RU
Highlight	.TW + NYH

Table Cloth & Ribbon

Base	.TW (very sparingly)
Shade	.PG
Tint	.CL + PG
Highlight	.TW

Background Drape

Base	.TW + PG + small amt. CL
. . . .	.Add NYH in some spots
Shade	.Base mix + PG
Highlight	.TW
Tint	.TW + NYH + AC

© 1989
Gretchen

Surface available from The Sawdust Makers, Box 4330, Sportman's Retreat, Onalaska, TX 77360, (409) 646-3121.

Grace & Charm

Flowers in Baskets

Red Tulips
Base.........FT + CRL
Shade ....CRL + AC
Highlight......TW
Tint ....TW + AC + FU

Purple Tulips
Base.........TW + AC + FU
Shade ....AC + FU + PG
Highlight......TW
Tint ....TW + AC

Filler Flowers
.............FU + AC + TW
.............TW + AC
.............TW

Leaves
.............CL + PG + TW

Tulips at Bottom of Box

Inside Tulip & Bud
Base.........FT + CRL
Shade ....CRL + AC
.............AC + PG
Highlight......TW

Outside Tulip
Dark Area .....CRL + FT
Light Area .....CL + TW + small
amt. NYH

Shade ....CRL + AC
.............AC + PG
Tint ....TW + AC + FU
Highlight......TW

Leaves
Base.........CL + PG + TW
Shade ....Base mix + BLK
Highlight......TW + CL
Tint ....Flower mixtures

Flowers on Initials
.............AC + FU + TW
.............CRL + FT
.............FT + TW

Reverse tulip pattern to fit other side of box.

Monarch Daisies

Monarch Daisies

This candle plate was painted with Terra Cotta acrylic by Ceramcoat. Do not paint the rim. Antique the plate with BMA, being sure to do the rim at the same time. Strengthen the antiquing along the inner edge of the rim with BU. Flyspeck with BU.

Daisies

Undercolor	BMA
Overcolor	CYD + YO
	CO + YO + small amt. CRL
Highlight	CYL + NYL
Tint	BMA + GL + small amt. CRL

Start to build values within the petals by overstroking all of the petals with CYD + YO. Lighten some of the petals on the left flower with CYL + YO. Strengthen darker petals with CO + YO + CRL. Add additional highlights where needed and tints in the darkest areas.

Center

Base	BMA + GL
Shade	BU
Highlight	CO-CYD
Splotches	BU-Yellow

Leaves

Dark Area	BU + CYL
Mid Value	YO or RS or CRL
Light Area	CYL + small amt. BU
Highlight	CYL + TW-TW
Tint	BLK + TW
	Flower colors

Berries

Base	Light Leaf Green
Shade	BU
Highlight	TW
Tint	CO

Filler Flowers

	BMA-CO-CRL-CYD-NYL-BLK + TW

© 1985
Gretchen

Mauve Pansies

This turned box is painted with Ceramcoat Lichen Grey. The edges are gold leafed. The leaf border, at left, should be painted around the perimeter of box.

Top Pansy: Three Front Petals

Light Area

Base. . . . . .NYD
Shade . . . . .BLK + TW
Highlight. . . . . .TW
Tint . . . . .CYD-CRL

Dark Streaks

Base. . . . . .MAUVE
Shade . . . . .BLK

Light Streaks

. . . . .CYD

Top Pansy: Back Petals

Base. . . . . .BLK + TW
Shade . . . . .BLK
Highlight. . . . . .TW
Tint . . . . .NYD
. . . . .MAUVE + GL

Bottom Pansy: Front Petal

Light Area

Base. . . . . .BLK + TW
Shade . . . . .BLK
Highlight. . . . . .TW
. . . . .PB + TW
Tint . . . . .GL-GL +
MAUVE

Dark Streaks

. . . . .BLK

Light Streaks

. . . . .CRL

Box available from Cozad's, 316 Six Flags Mall, Arlington, TX 76011, (817) 649-3353.

Bottom Pansy: Back Petals

Base. . . . . .BLK + TW + PB
Shade . . . . .BLK
Tint . . . . .GL
Highlight. . . . . .TW

Leaves

Base. . . . . .BLK +
CYL + TW
Shade . . . . .Mix + BLK or
Mix + PB
Highlight. . . . . .TW
Tint . . . . .YO-Flower
colors

©1985

Victorian Charmers

Victorian shelf available from
The Picket Fence,
1308 North 9th St., Monette, Mo 65708,
(417) 235-5444

Victorian Charmers

These charming little birds look very Victorian when placed on Accent Country Colors Off-White acrylic and antiqued around the edges with a soft blue. For a more country look, change the background to Accent Country Colors Antique White. After spray sealing with Matte Finish, antique behind the birds with FU + P-G + TW. Keep the color more intense and darker in value between the daisies and the birds. Allow the color to fade to the left by adding more white and then softening into the background.

Birds

Eye and Beak

Base. . . . . . .BLK
Highlight . . .TW

Ring Around Eye

. . . . .TW

Head & Back

Base. . . . . . .TW + FU + PB +
              BLK (Mid value blue)
Shade . . . . .PB + BLK
Highlight . . .TW

Wing

Dark Area . .PG + BU
Light Area . .Dirty White

Tail

Dark Area . .PB + PG + TW
Light Area . .TW + PB + PG
Shade . . . . .BLK
Highlight . . .TW

Breast

Base. . . . . . .CO + RS
Shade . . . . .AC + BS-BU
Highlight . . .CL + NYH + TW
. . . . .CL + TW
. . . . .TW
Build highlights in steps, laying in the first color, blending, applying the second color, blending, etc.
Tint . . . . . . .TW + PG (when dry)

Branch

Base. . . . . . .RS
Shade . . . . .BU

Daisies

Undercolor. .BLK + BU
Overstroke. .TW + NYH + small
           amt. CL

Highlight . . .TW
Tint . . . . . . .YO + CO
. . . . .YO + CL
. . . . .TW + PG
. . . . .TW + PG + FU

Keep large daisies brighter with stronger accents. The underneath daisies should be grayer and cooler.

Daisy Centers

Base. . . . . . .YO + NYH
Shade . . . . .AC + BS
Highlight . . .TW + CL
. . . . .TW
Tint . . . . . . .CO + RS
. . . . .FU + TW
(when dry)

Pollen . . . . .BLK
. . . . .FU + TW
. . . . .TW

Trumpet Flowers

Base. . . . . . .NYH
Shade . . . .RS + CO
. . . . .BU + AC
Highlight . . .TW + CL
. . . . .TW
Tint . . . . . . .CO
. . . . .AC + FU
. . . . .TW + BLK (when dry)

Leaves

Base. . . . . . .CL + TW + BLK
Shade . . . . .Base mix + BLK
. . . . .PG
Highlight . . .TW + CL
. . . . .TW
Tint . . . . . . .PB + TW

A
Bounty
of
Blooms

Anemones & Butterflies

Daisies
Undercolor .....BLK+FU

Anemones
Light Area ......TW+FU+CoVH+
　　　　　　　small amt. BLK
Dark Area.......Light mix+FU+
　　　　　　　CoVH+BLK

Daisies
Overstroke ......TW+NYH

Anemones
Shade ....BLK+FU+CoVH

Daisies
Shade ....CoVH+BLK
　　　　　　　FU+BLK

Anemones
Highlight ....TW
Tint ....AC+FU+CoVH

Daisies
Highlight ....TW
Tint.................Flower colors

Anemones
Light Streaks ..TW

Votive ring and candle box with butterflies are available from The Sawdust Makers, 4330 Sportsman's Retreat, Onalaska TX 77360, (409) 646-3121.

Anemones & Butterflies

A fancy cut candle box and votive ring can add a distinctive touch to any area. They become extra special when you add a porcelain butterfly.

Background

Seal with Designs From the Heart Wood Sealer. Paint the outside with Delta Drizzle Grey and the inside with FolkArt Frosted Berry. Spray with Krylon Matte Finish before transferring the pattern.

Palette

Winsor & Newton Titanium White, Ivory Black, French Ultramarine, Cobalt Violet Hue, Naples Yellow Hue, Alizarin Crimson and Cadmium Lemon.

Butterflies

Apply TW + FU + CoVH and a small amount of turpentine next to the body and between the wings. With a dry brush, blend to the outer edge of the wings, keeping wing tips lighter. Apply a tint of TW + NYH to the wing tips. Base the body with BLK.

Daisies

Undercolor . . . . .BLK + FU
Overstroke. . . . .TW + NYH

Shade . . . . .CoVH + BLK
. . . . .FU + BLK
Highlight. . . . . .TW
Tint . . . . .Flower colors

Daisy Centers

Base. . . . . .NYH
Shade . . . . .AC + CoVH
Highlight. . . . . .TW
Pollen Dots . . . .BLK
. . . . .BLK + FU

Anemones

Light Area . . . . .TW + FU +
CoVH + small
amt. of BLK
Dark Area . . . . .Light mix + FU
+ CoVH
Shade . . . . .BLK + FU +
CoVH
Highlight. . . . . .TW
Tint . . . . .AC + FU +
CoVH
Light Streaks . . .TW

Pull the shaded area to form
streaks over the light area. When
nearly dry, pull light streaks into the
lower edge of the dark area.

Anemone Centers

Base. . . . . .BLK + FU
Highlight. . . . . .TW + FU +
CoVH
Stamens . . . . . .TW + BLK
Pollen Dots . . . .AC + TW

Leaves

Base. . . . . .TW + CL +
FU + BLK
Shade . . . . .CL + BLK + FU
Highlight. . . . . .TW + BLK
. . . . .TW
Tint . . . . .CoVH + TW
. . . . .FU + TW

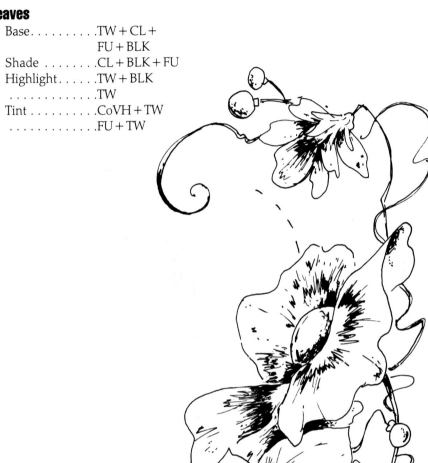

Country Love & Elegance

Lamb available from A "Couple" of Ideas, 8160 E. 44th St., Tulsa, OK 74145, (918) 664-2397.

Country Lace & Elegance

Base

Base

Highlight

Base

Shade

Shade

Tint

Highlight

Tint

Tint

Country Lace & Elegance

This life-size lamb painted with delicate flowers and lacy ribbon makes a stunning accent to a Country French room or to a little girl's bedroom. It is designed to hold dried flowers but will easily store magazines.

The background is painted with Accent Country Colors Antique White and is antiqued with BLK + TW.

Lighter Blossom

Base . . . . . . .TW + YO + CL (pale beige)
Shade . . . . .RS + small amt. AC
. . . . .AC + BLK (in deepest overlaps)
Highlight . . .TW
Tint . . . . . . .FU + TW + BLK (pale blue-gray)
. . . . .CL + TW

Darker Blossom

Base . . . . . . .TW + YO + CL (slightly darker than top blossom)
Shade . . . . .AC + RS (Use more AC than on top blossom)
. . . . .AC + BLK
Highlight . . .TW
Tint . . . . . . .YO + CL

Flower Centers

Base . . . . . . .YO
Highlight . . .TW + small amt. CL
Pollen dots .TW
. . . . .TW + TO

Leaves

Base . . . . . . .BLK + CL + TW
Shade . . . . .Base mix + BLK or
. . . . .Base mix + BLK + AC
Highlight . . .CL + TW
. . . . .TW
Tint . . . . . . .FU + TW
. . . . .Pink flower colors
. . . . .YO

Use tints sparingly. Overall the leaves should be a very pale gray-green with little contrast.

Bell-shaped flowers

Base . . . . . . .TW + CL + YO
Shade . . . . .TW + BLK + FU
Highlight . . .TW
Tint . . . . . . .CRL + TW
. . . . .CL + BLK
Keep flowers soft and delicate.

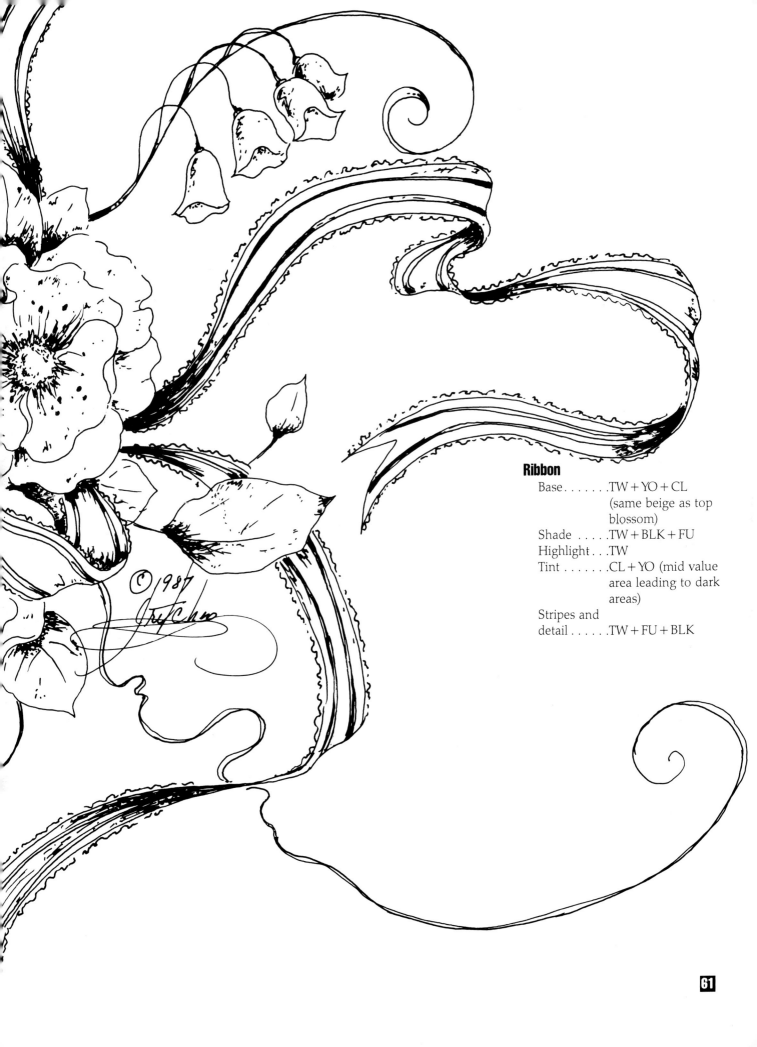

© 1987
[signature]

Ribbon

Base . . . . TW + YO + CL
(same beige as top
blossom)

Shade . . . . . TW + BLK + FU

Highlight . . . TW

Tint . . . . CL + YO (mid value
area leading to dark
areas)

Stripes and
detail . . . . . . TW + FU + BLK

Burgundy Blossoms

Burgundy Blossoms

Base
Shade

Dark Area
Mid Value
Light Area

Highlight

Shade
Highlight

Edge
Tint

Edge
Tint

Burgundy Blossoms

The richness of color in these blossoms comes partly from the stark contrast of the lighter blossom played against the strong burgundy blossom but also from the cool tints used throughout the flowers and the leaves.

Prepare the background with a wash of Accent Country Colors Off-White acrylic paint and water. The inset was painted with Quaker Grey acrylic. Antique behind the blossoms with PG + TW and add a few accents of LRO along the outer edges of the box.

Center Blossom

```
Base . . . . . . .TW + small amt.
                 NYH
Shade . . . . . .SG + BU
```

Highlight. . . .TW
Edge . . . . . . .FT-CRM-LRO
Tint . . . . .TW + BLK
. . . . .TW + DP

When placing color along the edge, start with FT edging in and then streaking from the outside edge. On some of the FT areas, continue to build stronger tints by streaking just a touch of CRM and then on some areas, LRO. Allow some areas to remain with the base color showing. Keep various values and intensities of color along this edge.

Left Blossom

Paint this the same as the center blossom, but along the edge add additional tints of LRO + AC so that the overall look is slightly darker.

Right Blossom

```
Dark Area . . . .AC + PG
Mid Value . . .CRM + LRO
Light Area. . . .FT + CRM
Shade . . . . . .PG + small amt. AC
Highlight. . . .FT-TW
Edge . . . . . . .AC + BU
Tint . . . . . . . .TW + DP
```

Flower Centers

```
Base . . . . . . .DP + BLK
Highlight. . . .TW + DP
Pollen . . . . . .BLK-TW + DP
```

Filler Flowers

```
. . . . . . . . . .TW-TW +
                 CL + BLK
```

Keep splotches very soft and barely visible against antiquing.

© 1989. *Hutcher*

Leaves

    Base . . . . .CL + TW + BLK
    Shade . . . . . . .Base mix + BLK
    Add DP to some.
    Highlight. . . .TW
    Tint . . . . .Flower colors

Berries

    Base . . . . .FT + CRM +
              AC + DP
    Vary values and colors.
    Shade . . . . . .DP + AC + small
              amt. PG
    Highlight. . . .TW + FT

Ribbon

    Base . . . . .TW + small amt.
              NYH
    Shade . . . . . .TW + CL + small
              amt. BLK (Pale
              gray-green)
    Highlight. . . .TW
    Tint . . . . .FT

Surface available from The Sawdust Maker,
Box 4330, Sportsmans Retreat, Onalaska, TX
77360, (409) 646-3121.

A Summer Nosegay

Background

Seal with Designs From the Heart Wood Sealer. When dry, sand the surface and then basecoat with Ceramcoat AC Flesh. Spray lightly with Krylon Matte Finish. The edges of the surface are leafed with red variegated gold leaf.

Palette

Winsor & Newton Alkyd Colours: Light Red Oxide, Rose Madder, Titanium White, Naples Yellow Hue, Flesh Tint, Ivory Black, Cadmium Orange, Cerulean Blue Hue and Cadmium Lemon.

Peony

Dark Area . . .LRO + RM
Light Area . . .Dark mix + TW
              + NYH + small
              amt. FT
Shade . . . . . .LRO + RM
. . . . .LRO + RM + BLK
Highlight. . . .TW + NYH
. . . . .TW
Tint . . . . .CO + RM
. . . . .BLK + TW
. . . . .CO + NYH

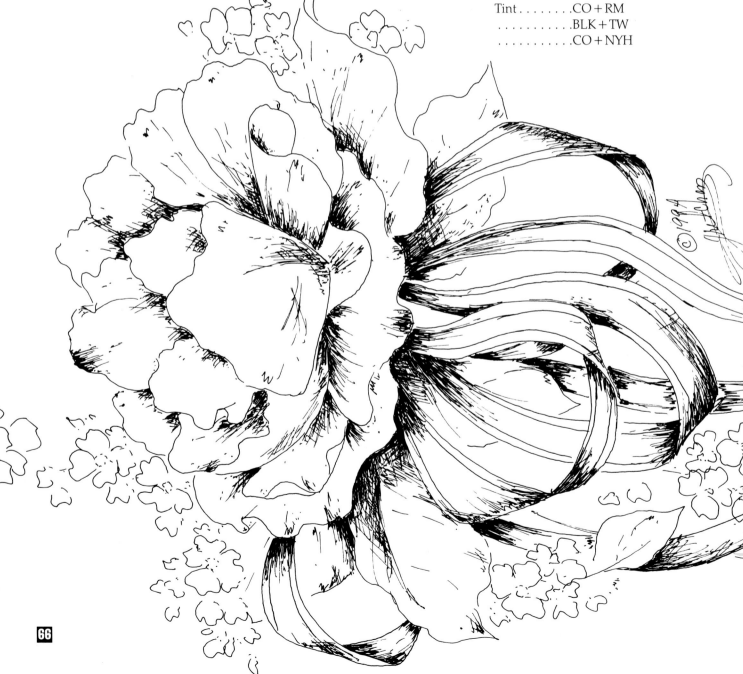

Ribbon

Base . . . . .NYH + TW
Shade . . . . . .LRO + RM
. . . . .CBH + RM +
          BLK + TW
Highlight. . . .TW
Tint . . . . .CBH + small amts.
          NYH & LRO
          (slightly grayish)
Stripe . . . . . .CBH + NYH +
          LRO

Leaves

Base . . . . . . .NYH + CL +
          BLK + TW
Shade . . . . . .Base + CBH +
          BLK
Highlight. . . .TW
Tint . . . . .RM
. . . . .CBM + TW

Filler Flowers

Base . . . . . . .TW + NYH
Shade . . . . . .Base + CBH +
          small amt.
          LRO + CO
Tint . . . . .CBH + RM + TW
          + small amt. BLK
Centers . . . . .CBH I RM
. . . . .CO

Apply dark and light values to the flower.
Base the ribbon and apply light value
shading in overlaps and strengthen with
deeper value.

Shade flower in the deepest overlaps and
where triangular corners form. Add tint
to the ribbon.

Highlight and add tints to
the flower. Highlight and
stripe the ribbon.

Base the flowers, then shade at the centers
and in overlaps. Apply tints and highlights
to the blossoms along outer edges. Add a few
suggestions of green leaves.

The Summer Nosegay surface is a̲v̲a̲i̲l̲a̲b̲l̲e̲ from The Sawdust Makers, 4330 Sport̲s̲m̲a̲n̲s̲ Retreat, Onalaska, TX 77360, (409) 646-̲X̲X̲X̲X̲

Woodland Lace

Ribbon
Dark Area.......FT+small amt. AC
Light Area ......TW+NYH

White Dogwood
Base ....TW+NYH
Shade ....BLK

Pink Dogwood
Base ....FT+TW+NYH
Shade ....FT+AC+small amt.BU

Ribbon
Shade ....FT+AC+BLK
Highlight ....TW

White Dogwood
Highlight ....TW
Tint.................FT+AC

Pink Dogwood
Shade ....BLK+TW
Highlight ....TW

Ribbon
Tint ....CBH+TW
Stripe..............CBH+TW

White Dogwood
Tint.................AC+BU
       TW+CBH

Pink Dogwood
Tint................FT+AC
       CBH+TW

*Woodland Lace mirror frame is
available from The Sawdust Makers,
4330 Sportsman's Retreat,
Onalaska, TX 77360,
(409) 646-3121.*

Woodland Lace

Dogwoods abound in the woodlands of eastern Oklahoma. In the spring, they form a canopy of lace and color, accenting the landscape with the glory of a new season.

Background

Seal with Designs From the Heart Wood Sealer. Paint with FolkArt Sachet Rose. When dry, apply a marbled background using FolkArt Dove Grey, Potpourri Rose and Wicker White. You will also need a natural sponge, DecoArt Control Medium and a large round brush.

Wet the sponge with water and dip it into the Control Medium and then barely dip it into the Dove Grey. Blot the sponge on paper and then dab. Drag the sponge diagonally across the surface, being sure to occasionally lift the sponge away from the background so that the paint application will be irregular. While the paint is still wet, use a brush dipped into a mixture of water and Control Medium and pull loose marble-like streaks through the paint. Additional paint may be added to the brush if necessary.

Repeat with each of the colors and then spray with Krylon Matte Finish.

Palette

Winsor & Newton Titanium White, Cadmium Lemon, Ivory Black, Naples Yellow Hue, Alizarin Crimson, Burnt Umber, Flesh Tint and Cerulean Blue Hue.

White Dogwoods

Base	TW + NYH
Shade	BLK
Highlight	TW
Tint	FT + AC
	AC + BU
	TW + CBH

Pink Dogwoods

Base	FT + TW + NYH
Shade	FT + AC + small amt. BU
	BLK + TW
Highlight	TW
Tint	FT + AC
	CBH + TW

Flower Center

Base	CL + BLK + CBH
Highlight	TW
Shade	BLK
Pollen Dots	NYH + TW

Leaves

Base	TW + CL + CBH + small amt. BLK
Shade	Base mix + BLK
Highlight	TW
	TW + CBH
Tint	AC + BU

Ribbon

Dark Area	.FT + small amt. AC
Light Area	.TW + NYH
Shade	.FT + AC + BLK
Highlight	.TW
Tint	.CBH + TW
Stripes	.CBH + TW

Spring Serenity

This wonderful dresser box with all its detail can dress up any vanity or bathroom counter. The hinged top, when opened, reveals a mirror and plenty of storage for all of your makeup.

Background

The lid, bottom trim and hearts were painted with two coats of White Lightning. The remaining portion of the box was washed with FolkArt Whipped Berry. Spray this area with Krylon Matte Finish and then antique with CoB + BLK + TW along the lower rim and at the corners.

Palette

Winsor & Newton Titanium White, Cobalt Violet Hue, Cobalt Blue, Ivory Black, Naples Yellow Hue, Cadmium Red Deep and Cadmium Lemon.

Upper Iris

Dark Area . . . . .CoVH + CoB + small amt. BLK
Light Area . . . . .TW + NYH
Tint . . . . .CoVH + CRD
Highlight. . . . . .TW

When placing in the dark areas, vary the color just slightly from petal to petal. Add additional BLK + CoB to the bottom center of the largest petal and on the two side petals. Other petals have more CoVH in them.

Lower Iris

Dark Area . . . . .CoB + CoVH + TW
Light Area. . . . .TW + NYH
Tint . . . . .CoVH + CRD
Shade . . . . .CoB + CoVH + BLK
Highlight. . . . . .TW

Apply shading in the overlaps on the upper extreme left and right petals at the tip of the center petal.

Beards

Base. . . . . .NYH
Shade . . . . .CRD
Highlight. . . . . .CL + TW

Leaves

Base. . . . . .TW + CL + BLK + CoB
Shade . . . . .Base mix + BLK + small amt. CoB
Highlight. . . . . .TW
Tint . . . . .Flower colors

Sky

Various mixtures of TW + CoB + BLK + CoVH. Keep the sky whiter over the top of the bridge and gray in the right corner.

Trees

Very light mixes of TW + BLK + CL + CoB. Allow background trees to be barely visible against the sky but darker at the ground line. Define the shape of the tall trees with stronger value changes.

Grass

Various values of TW + CL + BLK + CoB. Strengthen behind the iris with additional BLK.

Bridge

Base. . . . . .TW + BLK + CoB
Shade . . . . .Base mix + BLK
Highlight. . . . . .TW

Water

Base. . . . . .TW + CoB
Shade . . . . .Base mix + BLK + CoB
Highlight. . . . . .TW
Tint . . . . .TW + CoVH + CoB

Field Irises

Create stems at the bottom edge of each patch of irises by loading the brush with TW + CL + BLK + CoB and pulling up with the chisel edge of the brush. Using various mixtures of TW + CoB + CoVH, dab the suggestion of flowers on top of the stems. Keep the flowers less defined toward the back and bolder both in color and shape as you come forward.

Dresser box is available from
Wood You Imagine,
P. O. Box 691632,
Tulsa, OK 74169-1632.

Spring Serenity

Spring Serenity

Upper Iris

Dark Area.......CoVH+CoB+small amt. BLK
Light Area ......TW+NYH

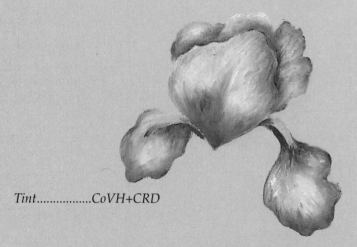

Tint................CoVH+CRD

Highlight........TW

Lower Iris

Dark Area.......CoB+CoVH+TW
Light Area ......TW+NYH

Tint................CoVH+CRD

Shade ....CoB+CoVH+BLK
Highlight........TW

Cornflower Blue

Cornflower Blue

This bowl was so much fun to paint since it was painted from the memory of my first visit to eastern Washington. In early spring the cornflowers bloom wild in the fields and pastures. They are a visual delight of soft pastels ranging from the softest pinks through the violets and into the blue color families.

The bowl was prepared with an off-white acrylic. Everything outside the oval was painted with Ceramcoat's Wedgewood Green. The trim was done in Ceramcoat's Salem Green. Antique the oval with OG + RS after spraying with Krylon Matte Finish.

Daisies

Undercolor . . . .OG + RS-YO
Overcolor . . . . .NYL + TW
Tint . . . . .NYD
. . . . .PB + BS + TW

Daisy Centers

Base. . . . . .NYD
Shade . . . . .RS + BMA
. . . . .BS
Highlight. . . . . .CYL + TW
. . . . .TW
Splotches. . . . . .RS + BLK

Cornflowers

Dark Area . . . . .PB + BS
Mid Value . . . . .BMA
Light Area. . . . .PB + BS + TW
Tint . . . . .BMA + TW
Shade . . . . .PB + BS

Cornflower Centers

Base. . . . . .BMA
Shade . . . . .BLK
Highlight. . . . . .TW or TW + PB

Wooden bowl is available from The Crafty Supplier, 904 S. Broadway, Little Rock, AR 72201, (501) 375-8653.

© 1984 Gretchen

Leaves

		or
Dark Area	BLK + COG + CYL	. . . . Dark mixture + BMA
Light Area	Dark mixture + CYL + TW	Highlight . . . . . . CYL + TW
Shade	Dark mixture + BLK or	. . . . BLK + TW
. . . .	Dark mixture + PB	Tint . . . . CYD-YO

The two drawer "mitten" chest is available from God's Country Store, P. O. Box 1491, Eagle River,WI 54521, (800) 342-1189.

Violets & Daisies

Violets & Daisies

Two floral favorites are combined with glossy ivy leaves to form a striking combination of deep purple violets and lavender-tinted daisies. The design is painted on a small two-drawer chest called a "mitten." Because this is a trailing pattern, it can be easily adapted to many surfaces.

Background

Seal with Designs From the Heart Wood Sealer and paint with Delta Light Ivory. Spray with Krylon Matte Finish before transferring the design.

Palette

Winsor & Newton Titanium White, Cadmium Lemon, Ivory Black, Naples Yellow Hue, Cobalt Violet Hue, Dioxazine Purple and Yellow Ochre.

Daisies

Undercolor	BLK + small amt. DP
Overstroke	TW + NYH
Shade	BLK + CoVH
Highlight	TW
Tint	CoVH + TW

Daisy Centers

Base	NYH + YO
Shade	DP
Highlight	TW + CL + NYH
	TW
Pollen Dots	BLK
	TW

Leaves

Base	CL + BLK + TW
Shade	Base mix + BLK
Highlight	CL + TW
	TW
Tint	TW + BLK

Keep the leaves very dark in their shaded areas. If necessary, add some DP. Use the same color to streak the leaves after all the painting steps have been completed. Apply the streaks in the same manner as you would the dark streaks on a pansy, being sure to follow the leaf contours. Do not streak the smaller leaves.

Violets

Base	Various mixes of CoVH + DP + BLK + TW
Throat	CL
Highlight	TW
Dark Streaks	BLK
Strokes	TW

Base the petals up to the yellow throats and complete the highlighting and shading before applying the yellow throats. Dark streaks extend from the lower edge of the yellow throat onto the purple area of the flowers. Do not allow the strokes to become too bright. If necessary, add a touch of BLK to gray them a bit.

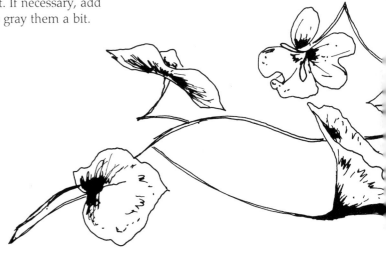

©1992 Gretchen

Old Fashioned Goodness

Bright and cheerful zinnias painted on a dough riser remind me of days long ago when my great grand-mother baked bread and always had it ready when we arrived. The dough riser for this project was prepared by removing rust and then painting the riser with a rust preventative spray. When dry, the riser was painted with several coats of Ceramcoat Antique White and the trim was painted with Butter Yellow. It was antiqued with RS + BLK + CYL.

The flowers were blocked in using the darkest color in a crescent form on the left side of the blossom. The right side was kept lighter. After the flower colors were blocked in and roughly blended, the pattern was placed over the flower and the petals were traced. Shading and highlighting developed the overlaps.

Lower Right Flower

Dark Area . . . . . CO + RS + LRO
Light Area . . . . . CO + RS
Shade . . . . RS + GL
Highlight . . . . . . CYD-CYL-
                      CYL + TW-TW
Tint . . . . CRL

Lower Center Flower

Dark Area . . . . . CRL + CO + YO
Mid Value . . . . . Dark mix + CO
Light Area . . . . . CO + YO
Shade . . . . GL + RS
Highlight . . . . . . CYL-CYL + TW
Tint . . . . CRL

Lower Left Flower

Dark Area . . . . . GL + RS
Light Area . . . . . CRL + RS
Shade . . . . GL + RS + BLK
Highlight . . . . . . CO + RS-CYD

Upper Left Flower

Dark Area . . . . . YO + CYD
Light Area . . . . . CYL
Shade . . . . YO-RS
Highlight . . . . . . CYL + TW-TW
Tint . . . . CRL + RS-CO

Upper Right Flower

Dark Area . . . . . CO
Light Area . . . . . CYD
Shade . . . . CRL + RS
Highlight . . . . . . CYL-CYL + TW

Flower Centers

Dark Area . . . . . BLK + RS
Light . . . . TW + TYG-TW
Tint . . . . CYD

Leaves

Dark Area . . . . . BLK +
                      CYL + TW
Mid Value . . . . . YO in some
                      leaves
Light Area . . . . . Dark mix +
                      CYL + TW
Shade . . . . Dark mix + BLK
                      or
. . . . Dark mix + GL
Highlight . . . . . . CYL + TW-TW
Tint . . . . Flower colors

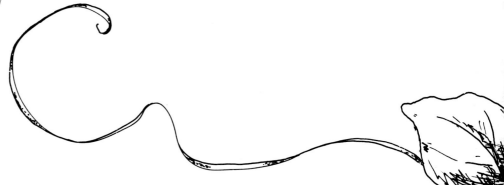

© 1985
JM Chew

Roses... Step-By-Step

Step 1—Make an egg-shaped area of dark value color in the center cupped area of the rose. Scratch a line to indicate where the front of the rose cuts across the cup.

Step 2—With dark area color on the brush, load one side of the brush into the lighter color. Keep this color dull and close to the background color in value. Blend color well on the palette so that there is no bold break between the two colors—only a soft, gradual change from dark to light. In order to get value change within these colors, do not paint too dry. On the other hand, try not to use so much paint that you leave ridges of color along the edges of the blending area.

Step 3—With lighter color on the upper edge of brush and dark color on the lower edge, flair a halo of petals across the upper edge of the egg. The first stroke should start on the chisel edge and then flatten as you pull across the top of the rose. Let the last stroke anchor to the right side with a chisel-edge stroke. Through the center area of the petals, press and lift the brush repeatedly to get a soft and delicate rose. Keep the top of the rose arched and high.

Step 4—Add additional lighter value color to the light side of the brush. Paint additional rows of petals, getting lighter in value as you come forward. It is not necessary that every petal and every row be well de-

fined. You need only give the illusion of many petals and rows of petals. Be sure to follow the arch you have already created. If the lower edge of the last row of petals is a bit hard and stiff, gently dry brush just along the lower edge. When applying these filler rows of petals, place more pressure on the upper, lighter colored edge of the brush.

Step 5—With the brush loaded as in step two, paint the front of the rose. Anchor to the left, pulling down on the chisel edge, and then continue across the front of the rose, pressing and lifting as you come around the bowl. Let up on the pressure and anchor to the right side of the rose with the chisel edge. Place more pressure on the upper, lighter edge of the brush. This step may be repeated to create several rows of petals before continuing on to step six. Be sure that each row of petals becomes lighter in value and slightly more intense. Place each one just below the last row completed.

Step 6—Make additional strokes very light and bright in value and intensity on the front of the bowl. Let strokes start at the flower center, stroke out to the left or to the right. Begin by pressing hard on the brush and then let up on the pressure, anchoring to the outer edge of the flower with the chisel edge. It is not necessary to make two strokes on each flower. Sometimes one is sufficient.

Step 7—Load the brush as in step two and make a side stroke on either side of the bowl to form the outer petals. Place dark to the inside and light to the outside. Start with the brush at about a 45-degree angle to the back of the rose, then press slightly, tucking the stroke next to the bowl. Wrap the stroke towards the bottom center, lifting to the chisel edge.

Step 8—Once again, load the brush as in step two and add a third stroke along the lower edge towards the center. This stroke can be pulled from the left or from the right. One or two additional short strokes may be added for filler petals.

Step 9—Deepen and shade the bowl and any overlapping triangular corners with shading colors, and highlight and tint edges as necessary. Blend carefully.

Step 10—Add a few filler petals with a double-loaded brush. Petals can be added on over-elongated side petals creating the effect of two petals rather than one. Be sure that the added petal is brighter and is set slightly lower than the original stroke. Finish some filler petals with a bright, intense chisel-edge stroke indicating that just a sliver is visibly wrapping to the front of the flower.

Step 11—Add pollen to the throat of the rose.

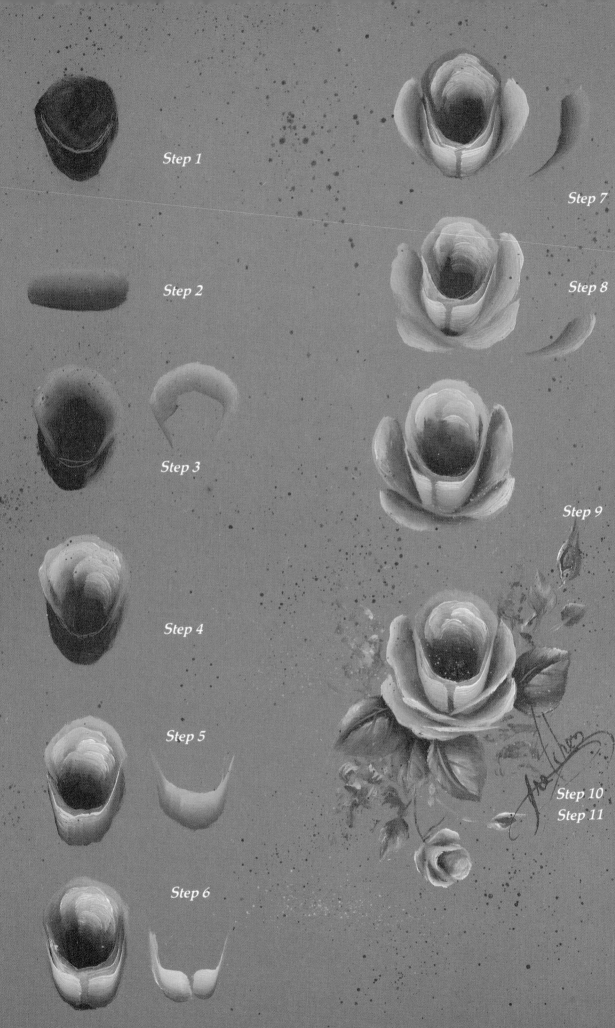

Step 1

Step 2

Step 3

Step 4

Step 5

Step 6

Step 7

Step 8

Step 9

Step 10

Step 11

Roses for Miss Mimi

The box is painted with Ceramcoat Wedgewood Green and Antique White. After you have finished painting the design, antique very softly on the inset with the rose colors.

Roses

Fluffy Base

Dark Area . . . . .GL + RS
Light Area . . . . .CRL + RS

Strokes

. . . . .CRL + YO + TW
    + small amt.
    CYL
. . . . .Above mix + TW
. . . . .NYL + TW

Daisies

Undercolor . . . .RS + BLK
Overcolor . . . . .TW + small amt.
    CYL
Tint . . . . .Rose mixtures

Centers

Base . . . . .YO
Shade . . . . .CRL + RS
Highlight . . . . . .CYL + TW
Splotches . . . . . .RS + BLK

Lily of the Valley

Base . . . . .NYL + small
    amt. CYL
Shade . . . . .BLK + CYL +
    NYL
Highlight . . . . . .TW
Tint . . . . .Rose mixtures

Leaves

Base . . . . .BLK +
    CYL + TW
Shade . . . . .Mix + BLK
Highlight . . . . . .TW
Tint . . . . .Flower colors

© 1995

Roses for Miss Mimi

Heart of Spring

Heart of Spring

The softness of this painting was achieved by the repetition of the background color throughout the painting. Notice that the lighter petals repeat this color as does the highlight in the trumpets and the leaves. Follow the diagrams for placement of colors.

The background is painted with Delta Old Parchment and is trimmed with Delta Terra Cotta. Spray seal with Krylon Matte Finish before painting. The background under the leaves is antiqued with the leaf green mixtures from the palette.

©1986

Base = B
Mid Value = M
Light Area = L
Dark Area = D
Shade = S
Tint = T
Highlight = X

Outer Petals

Base . . . . .NYL
Shade . . . . .CYL + YO + TYG
               + small amt.
               BLK
Highlight . . . . . .TW
Tint . . . . .Flower colors
. . . . .TYG

Leaves

Base . . . . .CYL +
               BLK + TW
Add TYG to some leaves.
Shade . . . . . . .Base mix + BLK
Highlight . . . . .BLK + TW
. . . . .TW
Tint . . . . .Flower colors

Trumpets

Dark Area . . . . .CRL + YO +
               CYD
Mid Value . . . . .CYD + YO
Light Area . . . . .NYL
Shade . . . . . . .AC + RS
Highlight . . . . . .TW
Tint . . . . .BLK + TW

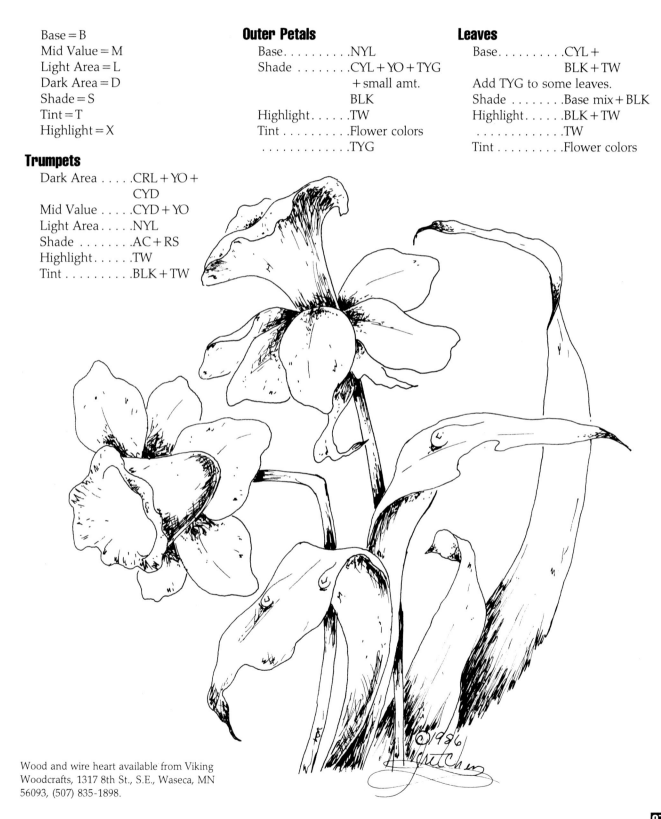

Wood and wire heart available from Viking Woodcrafts, 1317 8th St., S.E., Waseca, MN 56093, (507) 835-1898.

CHAPTER III

Fabulous Fruit

Crab Apples

Dark Area
Mid Value
Light Area

Shade

Highlight

Tint

Dark Area   Mid Value
Light Area

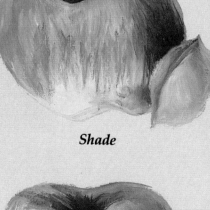

Shade

Highlight

Tint

Crab Apples

Crab Apples

The mood for this simple tray is set with soft pastel apples, just a touch of green and lots of warm pink. Paint the inset with FolkArt Vanilla Cream and the flange with Delta Stone Wedge. The flange is antiqued with TW + BLK where it meets the floor of the tray. When you have completed the painting, soften the background with TW + BLK around the core of the design, then add a few of the warm pink tones from the apples along the outer edge.

Top Apple

Dark Area . . . . . CRM + NYH
Mid Value . . . . . Dark mix + NYH
Light Area . . . . . TW + CL + SG
Shade . . . . AC + small amt. BLK
Highlight . . . . . . TW + small amt. CL
Tint . . . . TW + BLK (when dry)

Middle Apple

Dark Area . . . . . AC
Mid Value . . . . . CRM
Light Area . . . . . NYH + FT
Shade . . . . AC + small amt. BLK
Highlight . . . . . . TW + NYH
Tint . . . . TW + BLK

Bottom Apple

Dark Area . . . . . NYH + CRM
Mid Value . . . . . Dark mix + TW
Light Area . . . . . TW + CL + small amt. SG
Shade . . . . CRM + AC + small amt. BLK
Highlight . . . . . . TW
Tint . . . . TW + BLK (when dry)

Daisies

Undercolor . . . . BLK
Overcolor . . . . . TW + small amt. NYH
Highlight . . . . . . TW

Daisy Center

Base. . . . . .NYH
Shade . . . . .AC
Highlight. . . . . .TW
Pollen . . . . . . .BLK-TW

Ribbon

Base. . . . . .TW + NYH
Shade . . . . . . .CL + TW + BLK
Highlight. . . . . .TW
Stripes . . . . . . .CRM + TW

Leaves

Base. . . . . .CL + BLK + TW
Shade . . . . . . .Base mix + small
                   amt. BLK
Highlight. . . . . .TW

Apple tray available from A Couple of Ideas,
8160 E. 44th Street, Tulsa, OK 74145,
(918) 664-2397.

Block in Light, Mid, and Dark values on the apples and barely blend beginning to create streaks. Apply Dark and Light to the ribbon. Base the leaves and apply shading.

Apply first value highlight and shading blending to create strea on the apples. Highlight the lea and shade the ribbon.

Apply the final highlight to the apples and refine the streaking. Add the tint to the reflected light area and apply the freckles. Highlight the ribbon and apply tints. Brighten highlights on the leaves and add tints.

Cornish Apples

The Cornish Apple surface is available from
The Sawdust Makers, 4330 Sportsman's Retreat,
Onalaska, TX 77360, (409) 646-3121.

Cornish Apples

I spend the summer watching the fruit mature on the trees and wishing that I could pick off just one apple and enjoy its sweetness. Through the seasons, I watch the tree as it turns from winter's hard, bare branches to spring's beautiful, shapely boughs festooned with blossoms of unimagined beauty. It is difficult to understand how such a delicate blossom can produce heavy and luscious fruit to be enjoyed throughout the fall and winter months.

Background

Seal with Designs From the Heart Wood Sealer. Sand when dry and paint the back board with Ceramcoat Red Iron Oxide. Basecoat the top surface using Country Colors Wild Honey. When the basecoat is dry, spray lightly with Krylon Matte Finish. When the painting is complete, antique along the upper and lower edges of the painting surface with green colors from your palette and gold leaf with back board.

Palette

Winsor & Newton Alkyd Colours: Cadmium Lemon, Paynes Grey, Titanium White, Yellow Ochre, Cadmium Red Light, Cadmium Red Deep, Raw Umber, Naples Yellow Hue and Ivory Black.

Apples

Dark Area . . . . .CRL + CRD
Mid Value . . . . .YO + CRL
. . . . .YO
Light Area . . . . .YO + CL + PG
Shade . . . . .CRD + RU
Highlight. . . . . .CRL + NYH
. . . . .TW
Tint . . . . .TW + BLK
Freckles . . . . . . .Base with
                YO + CL + PG
. . . . .outline with RU

Ribbon

Dark Area . . . . .CRL + RU
Light Area . . . . .CRL + YO
Shade . . . . .CRD + RU
Highlight. . . . . .CRL + NYH
Tint . . . . .TW + BLK

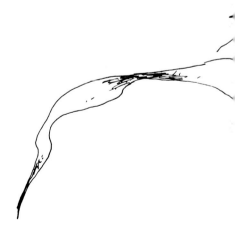

Leaves
Base.........CL + BLK +
                RU
Shade ....Base + BLK
............RU + CRD
Highlight.....CL + TW
Tint.........RU + CRD
............RU + CRL

Branch
Base.........RU
Highlight......CL + BLK

The Amish Sister Bowl

I have heard it is tradition for every Amish family to have these flat, round bowls available in a variety of sizes—from large to medium to small sizes. The largest bowl is given to the oldest sister in the family, the smallest bowl is given to the youngest sister, and the middle-size bowls are given to the middle sisters.

Prepare your Amish sister bowl by following the manufacturer's instructions. The surface should be painted with Delta Heritage Blue or Accent Country Colors Soldier Blue spray paint. If you're using the acrylic brush-on color, be sure to spray seal it with Krylon Matte Finish. When tracing the pattern, it is not necessary to trace every circle on the berries. Trace only one large circle for each berry. Antique under the lip of the bowl with FU + BLK. The interior of the bowl is painted with Delta Fire Red and then antiqued with AC + BU.

Plums

Dark Area	.BLK + FU + small amt. AC
Mid Value	.IR
Light Area	.Dark mix + TW (mid value blue-gray)
Shade	.BLK
Highlight	.TW + YO (left plum)
. . . .	.TW (right plum)
Tint	.CRM-CRL-CRL + CL
. . . .	.AC + IR (apply in mid value area)

Apply CRM to tint outer edge. Blend and then build brighter with CRL. Blend and then add a glint of CRL + CL.

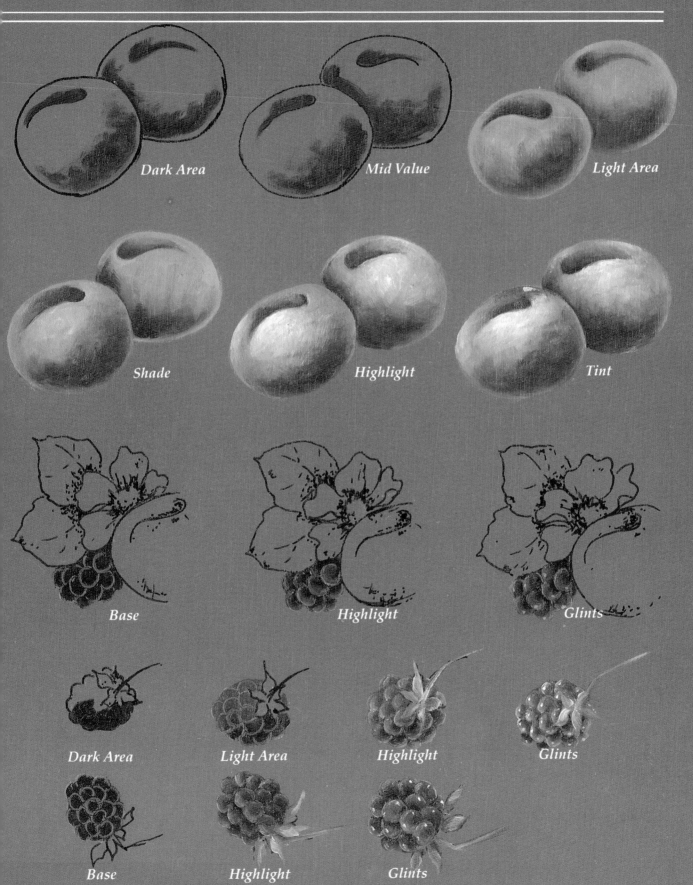

Dark Area

Mid Value

Light Area

Shade

Highlight

Tint

Base

Highlight

Glints

Dark Area

Light Area

Highlight

Glints

Base

Highlight

Glints

The Amish Sister Bowl

Blossoms

Base . . . . .TW + TO
Shade . . . . .BLK + AC + FU
Highlight . . . . . .TW
Tint . . . . .AC + FU + BLK

Be sure to keep the blossom on the left whiter and brighter than the blossom on the right.

Centers

Base . . . . .RS
Shade . . . . .IR-AC + BLK
Highlight . . . . . .CL + TW
Dots . . . . .BLK-FU + TW

Leaves

Base . . . . .CL + BLK + TW
Shade . . . . .Base mix + BLK
           or
. . . . .BLK + AC
Highlight . . . . .TW + BLK + FU
Tint . . . . .AC + BLK
. . . . .FU + TW
. . . . .Berry Colors

Keep the leaves cooler in tone. Do not allow them to become too yellow-green as this will distract from the plums and berries. Be sure that the highlights are blue-gray and that tints are pushed back into the darkest areas on most of the leaves.

Where the notes indicate that the berry is to be based, basecoat the entire berry with this color. If a light and a dark area are given, base the upper part of the berry light and the lower part dark, then using the handle of your brush or any other sharp instrument, scratch out the individual kernels and begin highlighting each kernel. As you highlight, be sure that the highlight color does not drift into the dark overlapping areas. This should remain the base color. The dots form glints on each berry.

Left Berry Under Plum

Base . . . . .AC + BLK
Highlight . . . . . .IR-FU +
 TW + BLK
Glints . . . . .FU + TW
Highlight each kernel with IR
and then re-highlight with FU + TW
+ BLK.

Left Center and Lower Right Berry

Dark Area . . . . .AC + BLK
Light Area . . . . .IR
Highlight . . . . . .CRL-CL + TW
 (light side)
 . . . . .FU + TW
 (dark side)

Glints . . . . .CL + TW
 (light side)
 . . . . .FU + TW
 (dark side)

Extreme Left and Upper Right Berry

Base . . . . .AC
Highlight . . . . . .CRM
 (each kernel)
 . . . . .AC + TW
 (light side)
 . . . . .FU + TW
 (dark side)
Glints . . . . .CL + TW
 (light side)

 . . . . .FU + TW
 (dark side)
Inner part of
berry . . . . .FU + BLK

Ribbon

Base . . . . .TW + FU + BLK
Shade . . . . .FU + BLK + AC
Highlight . . . . . .TW + YO-TW
Stripe . . . . .TW + FU

Stem

Base . . . . .RS + BLK
Shade . . . . .BLK
Highlight . . . . . .CL + TW

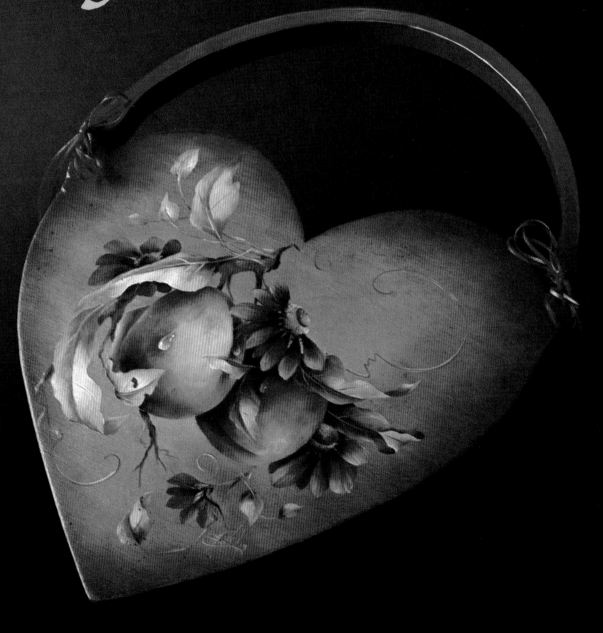

Deep Toned Peaches

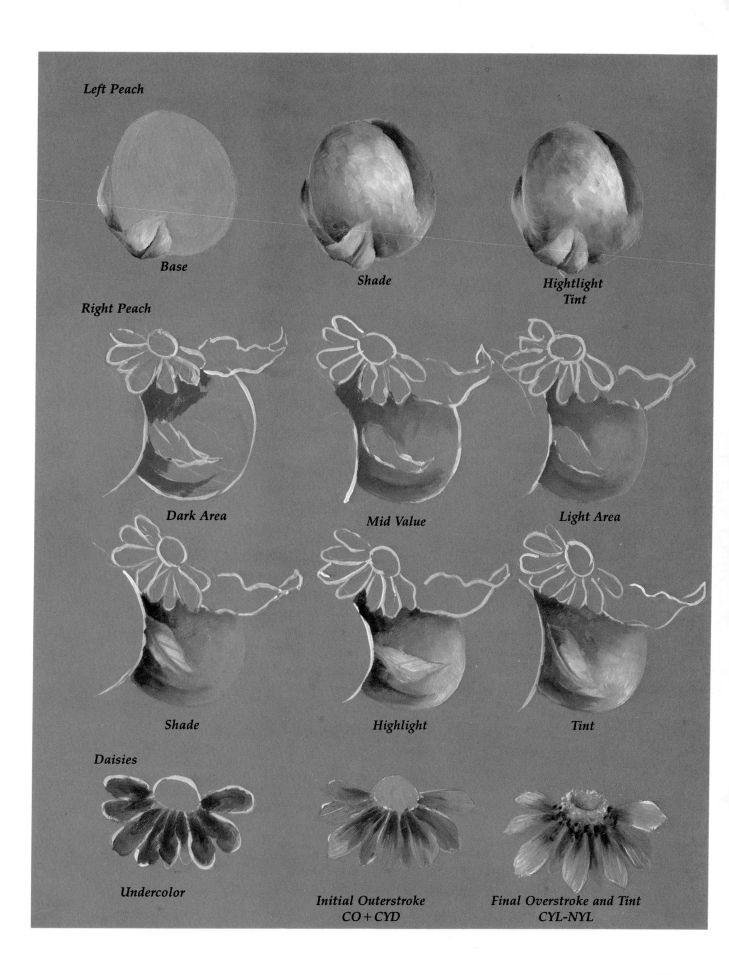

Left Peach

Base

Shade

Hightlight
Tint

Right Peach

Dark Area

Mid Value

Light Area

Shade

Highlight

Tint

Daisies

Undercolor

Initial Outerstroke
CO + CYD

Final Overstroke and Tint
CYL-NYL

113

Deep Toned Peaches

Create the look of color-on-color for a smashing and dramatic painting. It is important that you repeat not only the background color but the background values of the painting within the design elements. Note that the gold background is very close in value to the lighter peach, but that the antiquing picks up the darker values of the painting.

Prepare the surface with Delta Antique Gold acrylic. After spray sealing with Krylon Matte Finish, antique the edges with Burnt Umber plus Venetian Red. You may also add a small amount of Geranium Lake if the color looks a bit dull. Be cautious with the antiquing. It is important that it not overpower the painting but complements the overall design. It should only serve to draw attention to the focal point of the design, those luscious deep toned peaches. Remember that additional antiquing can be added after completion of the painting if necessary.

Left Peach
    Base.........YO + CYD
    Shade ....RS + VR + GL
    ....RS + GL + BLK
    Highlight.....CYL + NYL
    ....TW
    Tint ....CO-CRL-
                 CRL + TW
    ....BLK + TW
                 (when dry)

Right Peach
    Dark Area .....RS + GL + VR
    Mid Value .....RS + CO
    Light Area.....YO + CYD
    Shade ....Dark mix + GL
                 + small amt.
                 BLK
    Highlight......CYL + NYL
    Tint ....CRL-CRL + YO-
                 TW + BLK
                 (when dry)

Daisies

Undercolor
    Dark Area .....VR + GL + BLK
    Light Area.....GL + VR

Overstroke
    ....CO-CYD-CYL-
                 NYL

Overstroke, building one color on top of another as listed. Keep the petals on the right side lighter in value and those on the left darker. To dull a too bright petal, overstroke with CO + YO.
    Tint ....BLK + TW
                 (when dry)

Daisy Centers
    Base.........YO
    Shade ....GL + VR-
                 GL + BLK
    Highlight.....CYL + TW
    Tint ....TW + BLK
                 (when dry)
    Dots ....BLK

Leaves
    Dark Area .....RS + CYL + BLK
    Mid Value .....YO-CRL
    Use one or the other in some of the leaves.
    Light Area.....Dark mix + CYL
                 + TW + small
                 amt. TYG in
                 some leaves.
    Shade ....Dark mix +
                 BLK + RS or
    ....Dark mix + GL

    Highlight.....Light mix +
                 TYG + CYL +
                 TW-TW or
    ....CYL + TW-TW
    Tint ....Peach and daisy
                 colors

Branch
    Base.........RS
    Shade ....RS + BLK
    Highlight.....TYG + CYL
                 + TW

Heart-shaped surface from The Sawdust Makers, Box 4330, Sportsmans Retreat, Onalaska, TX 77360, (409) 646-3121.

Apply Dark, Mid and Light
values, developing a few streaks.

Apply undercolor and then stroke
petals with the overcolor.

Shade between the petals and
highlight upper petals. Add tints.

Basecoat and shade
in overlaps.

Apply Shade and Highlight,
creating additional streaks.

Highlight and add tin

116

Strengthen Highlight and Shading.
Add tints to the reflected light area.

Pick of the Season

*The heart panel is available from The Sawdust Makers,
4330 Sportsmans Retreat, Onalaska, TX 77360,
(409) 646-3121.*

Pick of the Season

Background

Seal with Designs From the Heart Wood Sealer. Sand when dry. Basecoat the inset with FolkArt Dove Grey. Spray lightly with Krylon Matte Finish. Apply several coats of White Lightning to the frame and lightly sand between coats. When dry, flyspeck the frame with gray colors from the palette.

Palette

Winsor & Newton Alkyd Colours: Paynes Grey, Titanium White, Naples Yellow Hue, Sap Green, Cadmium Lemon, Alizarin Crimson, Dioxazine Purple, Cadmium Red Medium, Cadmium Red Deep and Raw Umber.

Basket

Base	TW + NYH
Shade	RU + PG
Highlight	TW
Tint	NYH + CRM

Left Apple in Basket and on Table

Dark	CRM
Medium	CRM + TW
Light	CL + SG + TW
Shade	AC + DP
Highlight	TW
Tint	PG + TW + DP

Center Apple in Basket

Base	CRM
Shade	AC + DP
Highlight	AC + TW
Tint	TW + PG + DP

Right Apple in Basket

Base	CRD
Shade	AC + DP
Highlight	AC + TW
Tint	TW + PG + DP

Right Apple on Table

Dark	CRD
Medium	CRM
Light	SG + CL + small amt. TW
Shade	AC + CRD + DP
Highlight	CRM + TW
Tint	TW + PG + DP

Using apple colors, fill in the area between the basket weaves. Be sure to vary the values, creating stronger, darker shadows to form the apples tucked deep into the basket.

Daisy

Undercolor	PG
Overcolor	TW + NYH
Shade	PG
Highlight	TW
Tint	CRM + NYH

Daisy Centers

Base	SG + CL + TW
Shade	AC + DP
Highlight	TW
Tint	DP + TW
Pollen	BLK

Leaves

Base	CL + PG + TW
Shade	Base mix + PG
Highlight	TW
Tint	PG + TW
	AC + DP

Ribbon

Base	TW + NYH
Shade	PG
Highlight	TW
Tint	CRM + NYH
Stripe	CRM + AC

Resting Area

	PG, PG + TW, apple colors, leaf colors

© 1994

Bowl is available from Weston Bowl Mill, Rt. 100, Weston, VT 05161

Golden Delicious

Golden Delicious

This large bowl was painted with Delta Old Parchment and trimmed with Butter Yellow. When you are finished painting, antique behind the fruit with your palette colors.

Lightest Apples

Dark Area . . . . . YO
Mid Value . . . . . YO + NY
. . . . NY + CYL
Light Area . . . . . CYL + TW
Shade . . . . CRL + RS
. . . . DP + RS
Highlight . . . . . . TW
Tint . . . . CRL

Darkest Apple

Dark Area . . . . . RS + YO
Mid Value . . . . . YO + NY
Light Area . . . . . CYL + NY
Shade . . . . RS + DP
Highlight . . . . . CYL-TW
Tint . . . . CO + TYG

Leaf #1

Dark Area . . . . . BLK + CYL
Light Area . . . . . Dark mixture +
CYL + TW
Shade . . . . Dark mixture +
BLK
Highlight . . . . . . TW

Leaf #2

Base . . . . BLK + TW
Shade . . . . Base mixture +
BLK
Highlight . . . . . . TW

Leaf #3

Dark Area . . . . . RS + DP
Light Area . . . . . TYG
Shade . . . . RS + DP + GL
Highlight . . . . . TW + TYG
. . . . TW

©1983
Gretchen

CHAPTER IV

All Things Country

Grown-up Soys

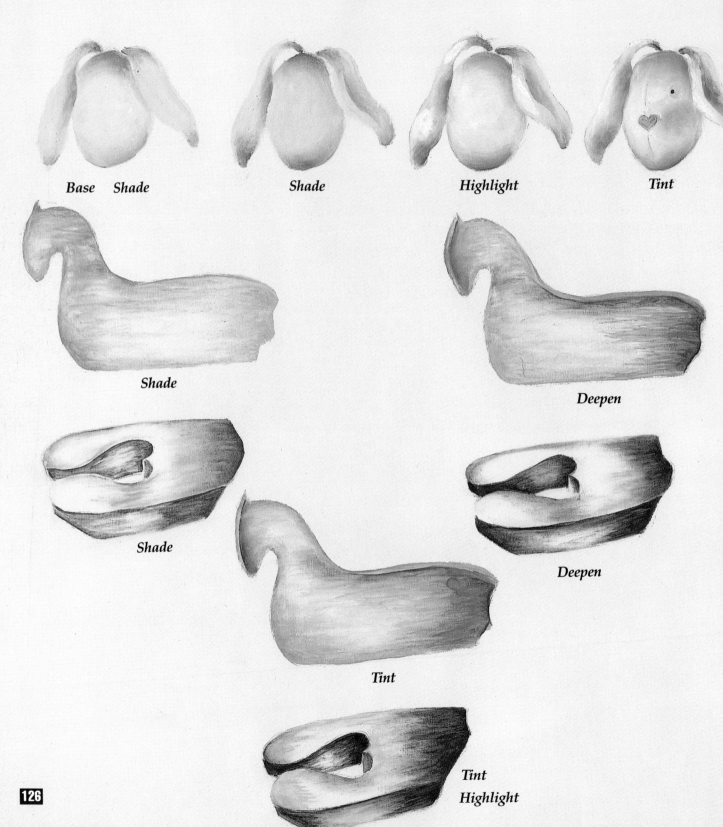

Base   Shade

Shade

Highlight

Tint

Shade

Deepen

Shade

Deepen

Tint

Tint
Highlight

Grown-up Toys

This simple still life, inspired by my collection of flea market finds, is quite easy to paint. Only the bunny and the ribbon are done in the traditional block-in and blended method. The heart and the rocking horse are painted by hazing color over the surface so that the background is visible through the paint.

The background is washed with an off-white acrylic paint and water so it will be transparent. Around the outside of the heart, apply a band of TW + CBH + YO. Keep the color a mid value blue-green. Using a tissue, soften antiquing away from the heart.

Bunny's Body
Base . . . . .TW + small amt.
                YO
Shade . . . . .RS-RU
Highlight . . . . . .TW
Tint . . . . .TW + DP + BS
                (in ears only)

Nose & Cheeks
. . . . .TW + CRL +
                BS + DP

Bunny's Eye
Shadow . . . . . . .TW + CBH + YO
Eye . . . . .RU

Scarf
Base . . . . .TW + CBH + YO
                (pale blue)
Shade . . . . . . .RU
Highlight . . . . . .TW
Tint . . . . .YO
Stripes . . . . . . .TW + CBH + YO
. . . . .TW + BS + DP

Dress
Dark Area . . . . .CBH + YO + BS
Light Area . . . . .TW + CBH
Shade . . . . .BS + CBH
Highlight . . . . . .TW
Detail . . . . .BS + DP
. . . . .BS + DP + TW
. . . . .YO + CBH
Use color to make a flowered design.

Apron
Base . . . . .TW + YO
Shade . . . . .BS + RS-RU
Highlight . . . . . .TW

Pantaloon
Base . . . . .YO + TW
Shade . . . . .RS-RU
Highlight . . . . . .TW

Feet
Base . . . . .TW + YO
Shade . . . . .YO-RU
Highlight . . . . . .TW
Tint . . . . .TW + CBH + YO
Stripes . . . . . . .TW + CBH + BS

Pony
Shade . . . . .RU + TW
Tint . . . . .CBH + TW
Apply TW + RU next to the bunny and blend it out to a thin, transparent haze of color across the body. Place some of the color on the left of the pony and haze it out towards the center. Be sure the color is transparent so the background shows. Apply additional shading if needed to set the pony behind the bunny and to set up the body width at the top and along the left side of the pony.

Base of Pony
Shade . . . . .BS
Deepen . . . . . . .BU
Tint . . . . .CBH + TW
Highlight . . . . . .TW
Apply color in the same hazed method as used on the pony.

Ribbon
Base . . . . .TW + CBH + YO
Shade . . . . .CBH + BS
Highlight . . . . . .TW

Resting Area
. . . . .RU-TW +
                CBH + YO

©1984

Heart box available from The Sawdust Makers,
Box 4330, Sportsmans Retreat, Onalaska, TX
77360, (409) 646-3121.

The Country Collection

This wonderful and delightful still life is filled with country momentos and can be easily and quickly painted when based with acrylic and then glazed with alkyds or oils and Winsor & Newton Blending and Glazing Medium.

The painting surface and the pegged area are painted with Ceram-Coat Fjord Blue. The white panels are painted with CeramCoat Antique White and then lightly stained with Burnt Umber.

Acrylic Painting

Weed pot. . . . . .ACF
Quilt . . . . .ACF
Block in the entire quilt and pillow area with ACF and then trace on the detail.
Hearts on side
panels . . . . .FB
Bands on weed
pot. . . . . .FB
Blue areas on the
pillow . . . . . . .FB
Rocking horse . .C
Red areas on the
pillow C
Yellow areas on
the pillow . . . . .BY

Allow the paint to dry, then trace on all of the detail on the quilt and the strokework on the rocking horse. Do not trace in the filler flowers or stems. Only give yourself a guideline for these areas.

Alkyd Painting

Quilt

Shade . . . . .BS + FU
Hearts . . . . .CYM + CRM
(red hearts)
. . . . .FU + BS + TW
(blue hearts)
Center Squares .CYM + TW
Highlight . . . . . .TW

©1987

131

The Country Collection

Heart shaker shelf available from The Sawdust Makers, Box 4330, Sportsmans Retreat, Onalaska, TX 77360, (409) 646-3121.

Begin by streaking dry color over the quilt to give it an aged and slightly grayish look. Make the shading darker behind the horse. Next, set on the small bands forming the squares by shading next to the yellow center square. Keep the bands darker next to the center squares and fade out. The small center squares are a very pale yellow mixture. Be sure that these do not become too bright. Apply the color to each heart sparingly so they will have an aged appearance that is soft and fading into the background. A few accents of TW or TW + CYM can be added to each square.

Rocking Horse

Glaze over the acrylic surface with a very thin coat of Winsor & Newton Blending and Glazing Medium and then streak the barest amount of color over the wet medium.

Shade . . . . .BS

Streak from the outer edges and in the shaded areas as indicated on the pattern.

Deepen shading . . . .BS + FU

Highlight . . . . .YO + small amt. TW

Allow this area to tack up, then do strokework on the rocking horse.

Strokework on Rocking Horse

Blue flower heads. . .FU + BS + TW

Heart . . . . .CRM + CYM + TW

Highlight . . . . .CYM + TW

Shade. . . . . .AC + FU + BS

Linework . . . . .AC + FU + BS

Highlight . . . . .CRM + CYM

Tint . . . . .FU + BS + TW

Strokes in heart . . . .FU + BS + TW

Strokes around flower heads . . . . . FU + BS + TW

Large strokes around linework . . . CRM + CYM

Overstroke. . . . . . .FU + BS + TW

Strokes on flower heads . . . .
CRM + CYM

Pillow

Glaze with Winsor & Newton Blending and Glazing Medium + Burnt Umber. Remove any excess so that an antiqued look results.

Blue Patches

Highlight . . . . .FU + TW
Detail . . . . .CYM + TW

Red Patches

Highlight . . . . .CRM +
CYM + TW

Yellow Patches

Highlight . . . . .CYM + TW
Detail. . . . . .FU + BS + TW

White Patches

Highlight . . . . .TW + small
amt. CYM
Detail. . . . . .FU + BS + TW

Weed Pot

Glaze with Winsor & Newton Blending & Glazing Medium and then apply colors.
Shade. . . . . .FU + BS + TW
Highlight . . . . .YO + TW-TW

Blue Streaks

Highlight . . . . .TW

Weeds

Streak up from the edge of the pot with a mixture of BS + FU to form the stems. Pull a few lighter stems with BU + FU + TW. The flowers are done with a very dark mixture of TW + FU + BS, CRM + CYM and YO + CYM + TW. Keep them sparse and dull, allowing them to be barely visible on the background.

Foreground . . .FU + BS with tints
of subject matter
colors

Country Compote

The background for this unusual fruit scoop was stained with RU and then deepened with BU.

Orange

Dark Area . . . . .RS + CRL
Mid Value . . . . .CRL + CO
. . . . .CO
Light Area . . . . .CYD
Shade . . . . .RS + RU
Highlight. . . . . .CYL
. . . . .CYL + NYL
. . . . .TW
Tint . . . . .TYG

Navel

Base. . . . . .BLK + CYL
Highlight. . . . . .CYL + TW

Pear

Base. . . . . .YO + CYL + TYG
Shade . . . . . . .Base mix + RU
Highlight. . . . . .TYG +
. . . . CYL + TW
Tint . . . . .CRL + RS
. . . . .LRO

Plums

Base. . . . . .BLK + PB + TW
Shade . . . . . . .BLK
Highlight. . . . . .TW
Glints . . . . . . .LRO-CRL-CO
Tints . . . . .Mauve

Light Grapes

Dark Area . . . . .Mauve + BLK
Light Area . . . . .LRO
Shade . . . . . . .BLK
Highlight. . . . . .CRL-TW
Tint . . . . .CO-PB + TW

Dark Grapes

Base. . . . . .Mauve
Shade . . . . . . .BLK
Highlight. . . . . .LRO-CRL-TW
Tint . . . . .PB + TW
Glints . . . . . . .CO-CYD

Daisies

Undercolor . . . .RS + BLK-YO
Overcolor . . . . .TW + CYL

Daisy Centers

Base. . . . . .YO
Shade . . . . . . .LRO
Highlight. . . . . .CYL
Splotches. . . . . .BLK

Leaves

Base. . . . . .BLK +
. . . . CYL + TW
Shade . . . . . . .Base mix + BLK
Highlight. . . . . .CYL + TW-TW

© 1984 Gretchen

Dresser tray available from Beech Knoll Wood Products, P.O. Box 211, Romeo, MI 48065, (313) 781-2440.

Always an Ample Heart

The tray was stained with a mixture of Olive Green plus Burnt Umber oil paint. The trim was done with dark blue-green acrylic color.

Each of the items in this still life holds special memories. The old enamel pot was found in the potting shed of my grandmother's neighbor. It brings memories of carefree child hood days and the neighbor's gentle way with us kids. The copper heart was bought during a recent trip to New York City. It's a daily reminder of the fun times we had in the Big Apple. The decoy was bought at a crafts fair in the Ozarks last year and is one of my favorites.

When painting the heart, be sure to fuzz out the area behind the dried flowers so that it fades into the background. If you darken the background behind the flowers with BU prior to painting them, you will achieve additional depth and fullness to the design.

Enamel Pot

Dark Area . . . . .TW + YO + BU
Mid Value . . . . .Dark mix + TW
Light Area . . . . .TW
Shade . . . . .Dark mix + BU
Highlight . . . . . .TW

Allow pot to dry, then . . .

Tint . . . . .BMA + CO
Streaks . . . . . . .BU + TW + YO
Rust Spots . . . . .BS + BU

Lip and Handle

Base . . . . .UB + BU
Highlight . . . . . .TW

Heart

Dark Area . . . . .BMA + RS
Mid Value . . . . .LRO + small
amt. CO
Light Area . . . . .CO + RS
Shade . . . . .LRO + BU-BU

Highlight . . . . . .CYD + YO-
CYD + TW
Tint . . . . .UB + BU + TW

Dried Flowers

. . . . .RS-BMA-CO
. . . . .UB + BU + TW-
UB + TW-BU

Resting Areas

. . . . .BU-CO

Decoy

Head and Lower Back

Base . . . . .UB + YO +
TW + small amt.
BU
Highlight . . . . . .TW
Shade . . . . .Base mix + BU

Eye

Base . . . . .BMA + CO
Highlight . . . . . .CO
Center . . . . . . .BLK

Beak

Base . . . . .UB + BU + TW
Shade . . . . .BU
Highlight . . . . . .TW

Breast

Base . . . . .YO + TW
Shade . . . . .RS-BU
Highlight . . . . . .TW
Detail . . . . .BU + turp

Upper Back

Base . . . . .RS
Highlight . . . . . .CYD + YO-
CYD + TW
Shade . . . . .BU

Tail

Base . . . . .BU + UB
Highlight . . . . . .TW

Pedestal

Base . . . . .NYL
Shade . . . . .RS-RS + BU

Always an Ample Heart

Newton Memories

Newton Memories

Newton Memories

This design was painted on an artist sketchbook (size 11" × 14"), but would also work well on canvas. The sketchbook has a unique leather-like grain to the surface that gave this painting a more masculine appeal. The background was painted with Ceramcoat Mocha acrylic. The corners were antiqued with BU.

My thanks go to Margy Wentz, former executive director of the National Society of Tole and Decorative Painters, for allowing me to use her lovely pot in this still life.

Copper Container

Dark Area . . . . .LRO
Mid Value . . . . .LRO + CO
Light Area . . . . .LRO + CYD
Shade . . . . .BMA
. . . . .BMA + BU
Highlight . . . . . .CYD-CYL
                   + NYL-NYL
Tint . . . . .BLK + TW
Glints . . . . .CYL + TW-TW

Brass Fitting and Candle Stick

Base . . . . .YO + CO
Shade . . . . .BLK + RS + CYL
Highlight . . . . . .CYL-CYL + TW
Tint . . . . .CO
Glints . . . . .TW

Screws on Fitting

Base . . . . .PB + BS + TW
Highlight . . . . . .TW
Shade . . . . .BU

Candle

Base . . . . .YO + NYL
Shade . . . . .BS + PB +
                   TW + BU
Tint . . . . .YO-BLK + TW
Highlight . . . . . .TW

Wick

Base . . . . .BU
Highlight . . . . . .TW

Tin Cheese Mold and Tin Handle

Dark Area . . . . .PB + BS + TW
                   (gray mixture)
Light Area . . . . .Dark mix + TW
Shade . . . . .Dark mix +
                   BU + BLK
Highlight . . . . . .Light mix + TW
Tint . . . . .YO

Wooden Handle

Base . . . . .RS
Shade . . . . .BS + BU
Highlight . . . . . .NYL-TW

Flowers

Block in the stem areas first with splotchy RS, BU and YO. Pull stems up and out of this with the chisel edge of the brush. Pull some stems with NYL and NYD for a lighter value.

When doing the blossoms, start with the darker colors plus a small amount of turp or oil to make the mixture loose and slightly transparent. Be loose and free with your flowers so that some of the background shows. Tight, close color causes the flowers to look bulky and too heavy for the design. Use blossom colors in this order: NYH-NYD-NYL-TW + CYL-BLK + TW-CO.

Resting Area

. . . . .BR-BU

Apply the BLK + TW tints to the container when the painting is dry for a splotchy, old look. You might also do the same with the highlight color.

Index

More Great Books for Great Crafts!